MIND MAPPING

Easy Steps to Master Mind Mapping Techniques

(Using Mind Maps for Product Development)

Anthony Maldonado

Published by Sharon Lohan

© **Anthony Maldonado**

All Rights Reserved

Mind Mapping: Easy Steps to Master Mind Mapping Techniques (Using Mind Maps for Product Development)

ISBN 978-1-990334-59-7

All rights reserved. No part of this guide may be reproduced in any form without permission in writing from the publisher except in the case of brief quotations embodied in critical articles or reviews.

Legal & Disclaimer

The information contained in this book is not designed to replace or take the place of any form of medicine or professional medical advice. The information in this book has been provided for educational and entertainment purposes only.

The information contained in this book has been compiled from sources deemed reliable, and it is accurate to the best of the Author's knowledge; however, the Author cannot guarantee its accuracy and validity and cannot be held liable for any errors or omissions. Changes are periodically made to this book. You must consult your doctor or get professional medical advice before using any of the suggested remedies, techniques, or information in this book.

Upon using the information contained in this book, you agree to hold harmless the Author from and against any damages, costs, and expenses, including any legal fees potentially resulting from the application of any of the information provided by this guide. This disclaimer applies to any damages or injury caused by the use and application, whether directly or indirectly, of any advice or information presented, whether for breach of contract, tort, negligence, personal injury, criminal intent, or under any other cause of action.

You agree to accept all risks of using the information presented inside this book. You need to consult a professional medical practitioner in order to ensure you are both able and healthy enough to participate in this program.

Table of Contents

INTRODUCTION 1

CHAPTER 1: WHAT IS MIND MAPPING? 3

CHAPTER 2: WHAT IS MIND MAPPING? 14

CHAPTER 3: DECIDE AND ACHIEVE YOUR OBJECTIVES 16

CHAPTER 4: WHAT IS MIND MAPPING? 35

CHAPTER 5: WHAT ARE MIND MAPS? 49

CHAPTER 6: OVER RECENT YEARS, THE BEST MIND MAPPING MATERIALS. 56

CHAPTER 7: BUILDING MIND MAPS THE RIGHT WAY 78

CHAPTER 8: MIND MAPS – AN OVERVIEW 83

CHAPTER 9: HOW TO PERSONALIZE A MIND MAP 87

CHAPTER 10: THE CORRECT WAY TO MAKE A MIND MAP 97

CHAPTER 11: MIND MAP CREATING TECHNIQUES 110

CHAPTER 12: MIND MAPPING IN BUSINESS 118

CHAPTER 13: CREATIVITY BRINGING OUT THE BEST IN YOU 131

CHAPTER 14: GETTING STARTED 138

CHAPTER 15: USING COLORS AND IMAGES IN MIND MAPS 161

CHAPTER 16: THE S.M.A.R.T. PHILOSOPHY 166

CHAPTER 17: MIND MAP TECHNIQUES 171

CHAPTER 18: MIND MAP SOFTWARE 176

CONCLUSION 190

INTRODUCTION

Throughout a whole day people experience many different things. They encounter new people, new problems, solutions to those problems, and many more. What does this have to do with organizing your thoughts and ideas? Simple, because of these experiences lots of things go through our mind and if we don't organize our thoughts it can get us confused as to what to do or slow down our progress in other matters.

This book will help you deal with that problem of having to know what information to use at the right time. Throughout the book you will learn multiple ways of organizing your thoughts, of course these are not the only ways but they have been proven to be effective which is why I chose to use them as well. By reading this book you will be able to accomplish tasks more efficiently and even find spare time if that's what you're looking for.

But first of all why is it important to organize your thoughts? As said earlier we encounter a lot of different experiences throughout the day and this will cause our brains to store new information constantly. Of course the information that we process is important that's why organizing your thoughts will help the brain in a huge way. If your thoughts are not organized it will cause more stress on the brain which in turn will cause more stress to the body. I'm pretty sure you would not want that to happen right? So let us get started.

Chapter 1: What Is Mind Mapping?

A mind map normally revolves around a single concept or idea, which is represented as an image at the center of a blank page, from which associated ideas are added, such as words or parts of words and images. When drawing a mind map, you usually connect the major ideas to the central concept. The other ideas can then branch out from these. You can draw a mind map as either a simple diagram, especially when in a hurry, such as during a lecture, or a complex image when you have the time.

Mind mapping is a very effective technique that you can use to get information in and out of your brain easily. It is a logical and creative means to take and make notes that literally map your ideas. Interestingly, all mind maps have one thing in common; they are organized in a structural manner that spreads out from the center, and they all use images, words, colors, symbols, and lines in simple and brain-friendly concepts. The benefit of using mind mapping is that it converts a long and monotonous series of information into a memorable, colorful, and highly organized image that is compatible with your brain's natural way of functioning. One simple way you can understand the concept of mind mapping is to think of it as a city map. The main idea is represented by the city center, the main roads coming from the city center represent the key thoughts, the branches and subsidiary roads represent your secondary thoughts, etc. Special shapes and images can represent particularly relevant ideas or landmarks of special interests.

Now that we have an idea of what mind mapping is, let us look at the benefits of mind mapping.

Uses of Mind Mapping

Before you start learning the techniques used in mind mapping and how to apply it in your everyday life, it is important you understand its uses. Most writers especially use this tool when they encounter writer's block or when they experience trouble organizing their thoughts and ideas together. Here are some of the applications of mind mapping:

Taking Meeting Notes

Taking notes using a mind map is a great way to capture the ideas discussed in a meeting. This is especially because meetings are usually nonlinear and rarely do they follow a specific agenda. In most cases, they are normally filled with an exchange of information, ideas, and discussion of countless thoughts, all of which need to be captured. Text notes are technically linear, and this makes it hard to capture ideas discussed in meetings effectively, especially when the meeting is nonlinear.

Book Summaries

Mind maps are especially effective when making book summaries. Books, especially nonfiction ones, contain ideas and concepts that you need to capture when reading. If you love reading and you normally take notes on the way, you may have experienced the urge to add an extra concept to a particular idea on another piece of paper. Perhaps you wanted to refer to older notes to make a connection. This may be especially tricky if you are using text, and the ideas may lead to much-disorganized notes. Mind maps are great for summarizing information, like that found in books. You can flesh out ideas and concepts using branches to represent your main concepts with your notes and organize them for easier comprehension.

Project management

While there are several software applications and tools for the purpose of managing projects, you can use mind maps to manage and administer smaller projects. You can start by having your core idea represented as the main project, and then have the following branches set up:

- Budget
- People
- Deadline
- Resources
- Scope

These branches are the essentials of any project. As such, you can easily use a mind map with them to administer a project. After you set up these branches, you can then review them on a regular basis as you carry on with the project.

Studying

Mind maps can come in handy especially when you are studying. You can use them in two great ways: one, to make notes during lectures and while studying; and two, to connect the dots when preparing for exams and tests. When you already have a mind map of what you want to recall, you can easily connect the dots using the mind map to comprehend the material at a fundamental level. As such, you will find that you do not need to get the minor details in order to understand the concept. As long as you understand the big concepts and strokes, you can easily implement them (of course, with practice) and solve problems like a breeze.

Goal Setting

Everyone sets goals at one point in their lives. As with most people, you probably rely on pen and paper to write down your goals. This is not a bad idea. In fact, this technique has been around for centuries and has worked well for many people. However, there is a more effective way of setting your goals: through mind maps. A great reason to use mind maps to set goals is that they are memorable. Why? Because they use visualization, using images and diagrams. As you represent your goals on a page, you can see the outcomes in your mind. Visualizing your goals when setting them is very crucial for their implementation, and that is why mind maps are much more effective than note-taking on paper.

Problem-Solving

Various approaches are available for problem-solving, but a great method to use is the 5W + 1H outline where you ask yourself several questions that need to be answered, in particular:

- Who

- Where

- How

- What

- When

This is a great application of mind maps because as you branch out on each section, chances are high that you will find relationships between your answers. These can be easily pinpointed on a mind map. As you find answers to all these questions, you will find that the problem is getting clearer, which will enable the solution to become more apparent. To use mind mapping to solve a problem, let your problem be your main idea, and the questions to be represented by branches. Try to answer these questions individually, and as you find answers to each one of them, you will most likely come to a solution.

Brainstorming

The thing with brainstorming is that it usually involves an exchange of numerous ideas, and sometimes most of them may not make sense. As such, you can easily capture all the ideas on a mind map and then reorganize them later to come up with sensible concepts. We are going to expound on this later on.

Knowledge Management

Most people rely on taking notes on paper while reading in order to understand a particular topic. This can be very inefficient at times, especially when you want to recall something amidst all the paragraphs of text. It would be unfortunate and cumbersome to reread through all these notes while you can easily use a mind map to locate specific ideas on the relevant topic. Rather than using notes to capture information, use mind maps to add knowledge to your bank. Knowledge management can be especially easy and effective, particularly now with the availability of software-based mind maps. Take the example of creating a knowledge bank on business networking. There are plenty of PDF documents containing tips, text notes on amazing business networking books, and a mind map on business networking through social media. What is the best way to make a knowledge bank using all this scattered information in different formats and in different files? The trick is to have all this information centralized and tie it in one place. You can represent all this information with a single mind map that will function as your knowledge bank. You can even manage this information using branches in mind maps in a structured way and in an easy format that will be simple to review.

Getting Things Done

While mind maps may be great when it comes to representing information in an easy format for easy recalling, they are admittedly not as probable when making a to-do list. You are more likely to benefit from pen and paper in that department. However, that does not mean you cannot use mind maps to get things done. Mind maps can be very beneficial, especially when you use a productivity technique like agile results or when you represent your GTD horizons, map them on a mind map, and then transfer the tasks to your task manager.

Decision-Making

Whenever you are faced with a circumstance that warrants making a decision, it always helps to have a range of options to choose from. You can benefit from either of two options: pen and paper or mind maps. While all these methods involve mapping out the options on paper, the distinction in mind maps is that you can make the options visual for easy follow-up. This can make a world of difference especially when you are weighing different options. It is easy to spot associations between given options primarily because of its visual nature. This is especially the case when you map out the different scenarios, and it becomes easier to connect various options in order to figure out the best option.

We will talk about the specific ways on how to apply mind mapping in the different areas of your life in the subsequent chapters of this book. But before we can get there, let's take a quick look at the different mind mapping techniques that you can use for success in the different areas of your life before we can narrow it down to the specific areas of your life.

Chapter 2: What Is Mind Mapping?

A mind map normally revolves around a single concept or idea, which is represented as an image at the center of a blank page, from which associated ideas are added such as words or parts of words and images. When drawing a mind map, you usually connect the major ideas to the central concept. The other ideas can then branch out from these. You can draw a mind map as either a simple diagram, especially when in a hurry, such as during a lecture, or a complex image when you have the time.

Mind mapping is a very effective technique that you can use to get information in and out of your brain easily. It is a logical and creative means to take and make notes that literally maps your ideas. Interestingly, all mind maps have one thing in common; they are organized in a structural manner that spreads out from the center, and they all use images, words, colors, symbols and lines in simple and brain friendly concepts. The benefit of using mind mapping is that it converts a long and monotonous series of information into a memorable, colorful and highly organized image that is compatible with your brain's natural way of functioning. One simple way you can understand the concept of mind mapping is to think of it as a city map. The main idea is represented by the city center, the main roads coming from the city center represent the key thoughts, the branches and subsidiary roads represent your secondary thoughts, etc. Special shapes and images can represent particularly relevant ideas or landmarks of special interests.

Now that we have an idea of what mind mapping is, let us look at the benefits of mind mapping.

Chapter 3: Decide And Achieve Your Objectives

Whoever has a "why," which serves as a goal, a finality, can live with any "how."
Nietzsche

we call these moments when alone in our office, It is those moments when everything seems difficult to implement, those moments when we believe that everything is against our interests, our well-being, where we feel to be lost without knowing where to start for us by

exit...

Are you there? ... Good! Now create a mind card and take the time to branch it out...

Identify the conditions that encourage you to become discouraged.

Why set goals?

When we drive our car, why do we turn to the right or left? Why do we think we arrive on time? How do we know we have enough fuel? Why are we wearing a tie at this time?

Probably because we know who we are going to see, that we have been able to appreciate the distance which separates us from our meeting place and that we know the name of the city or the district.

We can also think that the object of this meeting has meaning for us and that it corresponds to Nietzsche's " why " as a reason for being, of justification, of what it represents for us.

As for " how, "it corresponds to "sense" as direction, orientation.

In short, we simply set ourselves a goal.

Setting goals means giving yourself meaning! It knows where we want to go and identifying the routes and resources that will allow us to get there.

For the company's employees, the objectives are

"Fixed" by the hierarchy or the shareholders, they are rarely negotiable. On the other hand, the means and the way in which we will get there are more in our area of control. It will be a question of focusing on the "how," while knowing that we will have everything to gain by understanding the merits of these objectives, i.e., the "why." Our actions will then be more harmonious and fairer because we will have understood their meaning.

What is freedom?!

The work of Victor Frankl is a real source of inspiration for those who wonder about what freedom is. Former survivor of concentration camps, his extreme experience of deprivation allowed him to clarify this concept dear to all of us.

He said in this regard that mental health is based on a certain degree of tension between what we have already achieved and what remains to be achieved. What man needs is not to live without tension but rather to strive towards a valid goal, to carry out a freely chosen task.

In this regard, it is said that the Buddha was asked by one of his disciples about the best way to live. The Buddha knew that this person was a musician and asked him the following question :

" How do you make your zither produce the best sound?". " The pupil then replied: "the strings should be neither too tight nor too loose." The Buddha then asked him to draw inspiration from his know-how in terms of an instrument for living rightly.

Why break my head and not take life as it comes?

What will happen if we do nothing? If we don't want anything? It will then be easier to talk about the results of our problems than to talk about how we are going to solve them.

It is, therefore, not the path of inertia that we offer you but the one that makes us discover our capacity to be able to act on our life, in order to provide adequate responses to our desire to evolve.

For that, some preliminary efforts are necessary, as each time when it is a question of responsibility.

But where do I start?

Beforehand, we invite you to clarify some simple questions that we know how to avoid, with a summary and shallow answers :

- What exactly do we want?

- When do we want to reach it?

- What are we able to give up for this, and what will we never give up?

It takes courage to really answer these questions because they will refer us to our obstacles, our limits, and certain undesirable effects resulting from the achievement of our objectives.

Take the time to respond, and we will have the feeling of taking charge of ourselves, of being in control of our existence and will look twice before accepting assistance, which very often serves different interests from ours.

Once I clarified my goals, should I go headlong?

Now let's raise our heads. What do we see? Others! Whether on the street, in our workplace, at home, we are not alone. We operate in a social and cultural context that we share with those around us.

Contextualizing our objective helps us to make it compatible with our environment. It also allows us to anticipate possible obstacles and identify resources.

" My problem is the lack of time ..."

For everyone, the day includes a capital of 24 hours. We have no choice but to spend it or invest it. Inefficiently setting goals, we perform a fundamental time management act that determines the performance and consistency of all our actions.

To save time, you have to invest it.

Why the goal remains a problem in the company?

It is clear that we prefer the logic of the firefighter called to extinguish a fire in a poorly designed building than that of the architect who will have pre-accident the disaster in the design of his plans. We place ourselves in some sort in a survival position.

Subject to constant pressure, we often favor action over reflection, often assimilated to "unproductive" time. In addition, emergency treatment generates rapid gratification, and therefore pleasure in obtaining a prompt result.

Perhaps it is time to call upon our capacities for anticipation and proactivity by discerning the urgent from the important ...

The predominance of the left brain

The tools proposed to deal with the objective are often quantitative and analysis (left brain): spreadsheet, histogram, matrix, diagram...

However, the notions of vision, visualization, globality (right brain) are essential to understand the objective.

How do it?

We will recall here the fundamentals that allow efficiency in the design of objectives.

By being specific, concrete, observable, and measurable, the objective will gain in precision and clarity. To be rich is too vague. Having an annual income of € 100,000 in two years makes it easier to imagine what remains to be done.

The right brain does not understand the negative form. It is this which allows us to visualize our objective. Repeating: "Tomorrow, I will not be late," will not happen to mobilize our resources. To bring about a real change, let's prefer "tomorrow, I'll by 8:15 am at the office ", the asserted form will better serve our purpose. In addition, it forces us to say what we want and not what we no longer want.

Similarly, if we are asked not to imagine a penguin on an ice floe with a mask and a snorkel, there is a good chance that this image will impose itself on us anyway.

Let us ask ourselves the question of knowing if the achievement of our objective lies in our control zone; otherwise, this will require negotiation or constant watch. "Being the best" is only a wish outside our area of influence, because we do not always know who our competitors are and what they are preparing. On the other hand, "exceeding our turnover by 20%" is a performance objective which depends on our control area.

Let us project ourselves into the situation where our objective is reached. How do we feel? What do we mean? What do we see? This sensory projection generates a reflexive loop on our present and promotes the mobilization of all our resources. It is a real body-feeling-spirit preparation that provides great energy.

It goes without saying that our objectives must be in harmony with our values, our ultimate goal in life (meta-objective). Otherwise, we are mortgaging every chance of success. We will always be in internal conflict, consciously, and above all, unconsciously. Our strategy will always be thwarted, and our efforts will exhaust us. All this to arrive at a state of ill-being.

Contextualizing our objective allows us to validate its realism and consistency. It is a question of identifying the people involved, the environment in which it takes place.

If we anticipate all the results that result from achieving our goal (personal, professional, family, community, etc.), we can then manage the consequences in advance, rather than waiting for them to occur.

Take the example of an apartment that perfectly matches what we have long wanted in terms of surface area, brightness, number of bedrooms, exhibition... Are we ready to give up our children's nanny for entrusting them to someone else? Are we willing to extend our transportation time to get to our workplace? And many other questions that we will have to answer before making commitments.

This comprehensive approach will save us a lot of problems. It will take place throughout our journey, taking into account an ever-changing context.

Let us be lucid in estimating the obstacles and resources, and imagine how we can get around the former and identify and dispose of the latter.

Let's set indicators of success. This lets us know when the goal has been reached.

The branches support information at this level, which responds to "I will have reached my objective when ...". The indicators are necessarily visible and often quantifiable.

A schedule is obviously essential, and it can take the form of a retro-planning, that is to say from the date envisaged for the achievement of the objective in order to be declined in successive stages for finally lead to the precise date of the first action to be taken.

It is said that to take the first step is to have already traveled half the way. Action often eliminates fear.

Like a good sailor, we will stay the course on the destination, always with great flexibility and a sense of opportunity, and like him, we will take the time to celebrate the stages and the finish with dignity. We will draw new energy from this celebration for new goals.

The mind map as a strategic tool

We would like to share with you a way to use the objective-themed mind map. Perhaps you will appropriate it as it is or adapts it, or even discover others more in harmony with your functioning. The most important thing is to feel comfortable in your job and to feel a sense of control, and especially not to be helpless in front of a blank page.

We propose here a pragmatic use of the heuristic map, which respects the fundamentals developed previously.

The development of a map allows us a rational, sensory, and visionary representation of our objective.

This appropriation of the objective, according to a body-feelings-spirit approach, generates a strong motivation and induces a state of just and constant tension.

For this, we will take an example that Chris, a sales executive in a life insurance company wishing to be more efficient in his activity, given the new objectives that have been set for him in terms of turnover.

Clarify the objective

Chris knows that he must first be clear about his aspirations. He makes the first map with two branches: one represents what he no longer wants and the other what he wants to achieve.

The specific, concrete, observable, and measurable aspect will be respected for both branches.

Eventually, each branch will be assigned a code that will allow Chris to know if he is or is not in his control zone.

By relying on what he no longer wants, Chris finds more easily what he really wants. He thus identifies the indicators of his success.

ramify

Chris can then branch out all that he has positively formulated in his wishes by the sensory representation of what he will feel when he reaches them.

The quality of this work is based on his ability to live by evocation, a future state in his head, and in his body, thanks to the emotions he will be able to generate.

Words and drawings can evoke emotions, feelings, behaviors ... At this point, what should represent the heart of the map will emerge on its own. In from him, just find a beginning, an inspiration. This is the origin of all the ramifications.

Check

It is a question of ensuring if the objective itself and the path likely to reach it are compatible with the values of Chris and its environment.

For this, the first level branch "respect" is branched by a second-level "values" for which Chris does not compromise. The ramifications reflect the actions and tangible consequences resulting from respect for its values.

The second branch of the second level is devoted to the "environment" of Chris. The ramifications evoke the context in which he finds himself and his objective by answering the following questions: Where and with whom?

The anticipations linked to the consequences due to the achievement of its objectives concerning people and the environment are subject to ramifications.

Two new first-level branches discern the necessary resources (third branch) and the foreseeable obstacles (fourth branch). The ramifications allow Chris to develop the appropriate tactics to appropriate the resources and bypass or even anticipate obstacles. Chris's vigilance leads to constant updating of this branch.

A fifth branch of the first level is devoted to the staggering of tasks. This same branch has for the title the date that Chris chose to reach his goal or the one imposed on him by his management.

Each of the ramifications contains the nature of the task to be accomplished and its deadline, the persons concerned, or the resources to be implemented. Chris can highlight, cross out, or check off when he has done so.

A sixth, first-level branch allows Chris to collect the various events or information likely to modify its strategy. He will thus keep his memory of it, which could be useful for him in the event of restitution to his hierarchy. Keeping the history of these events also reminds him of the meaning (the why and the how) of his action.

Finally, on the seventh branch of the first level, Chris decides in advance of the rewards that he will grant himself or that he will receive as he progresses. This branch is considered by Chris to be as important as the others because it allows him to draw energy from it. It applies to the fact that the information it contains is most explicit on the sensory level (colors, volume, relief, emotions, etc.).

Value-added heuristic map

Although we have sequenced the phases of the user manual for the clarity of the demonstration, each branch can be branched independently of each other according to the availability of the information it must contain. A map can thus be easily updated, simply by removing or adding ramifications.

We recommend keeping all the cards that will be produced for the same purpose. This allows us to consult the history of our progress and assess its progress.

The global vision of all the components of our map invites us to identify the priorities and the simultaneity of certain actions more easily.

The more expressive, pictorial, and highlighted our map is, the easier it is to reactivate the anchors inducing the will to reach the goal.

In the example of the use of a map when we are lost, the mind map provides, through its clarity, a sense of serenity that allows us to keep cool head whatever the unforeseen and ambient pressure.

variations method

A goal can be collective. In this case, the method remains the same. We recommend that you invite each participant to prepare a card beforehand. Then, a facilitator consolidates all of the cards into one, promoting listening and discussion between participants.

Finally, the use of the mind map as part of coaching allows for reworking on the materials of the previous sessions and for preparing the following interviews. For this, a copy of the card is made available to the coach and the coachee after each appointment.

CHAPTER 4: WHAT IS MIND MAPPING?

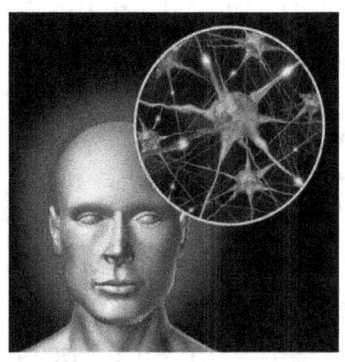

Brain maps have been utilized by the absolute most prominent personalities in history for a considerable length of time. Figuring out how to utilize mind maps consistently can immeasurably improve different limits throughout your life and your business. In this manner, it is certainly justified regardless of your opportunity to figure out how to make mind guides and use them successfully.

Psyche Mapping can be viewed as demonstration of distinguishing and naming our considerations and thoughts. At times this even incorporates our feelings also. When distinguished, you can mastermind them in various leveled order. This is an intriguing thought since they seem, by all accounts, to be non-hierarchal, however they are really organized in a progressive system structure, which can be very helpful.

To make a psyche map, you start with a focal subject, and afterward you move outward towards related points. From those points you can advance further into other related subtopics. Once in a while there are connections between the subtopics, so you will discover them cross referring to one another. Once in a while you will discover these subcategories circling again into each other such this is like how stream outlines work. This eventually permits you to hieratically organize your substance, however so that you can all the more likely imagine it.

Brain maps help you to outwardly take in the requesting and grouping of data, regardless of whether it is realities, information, or thoughts that you are attempting to break separated. An incredible method to consider a brain map is to consider it a planetary framework, the sun being the main issue which is being circled via planets. Every planet is additionally being circled by its own moon. This brisk perception permits you to consider the data in a three-dimensional arrangement.

One thing that is fascinating about brain maps is that they are a lot of lined up with what you would check whether you could investigate somebody's psyche. The cerebrum works likewise where one idea or memory is associated with another in a precise framework, for example, this. For instance, if you somehow happened to see a clasp of a superman film that you saw as a youngster, you may associate that memory with a toy that you were playing with at the time you saw that, and as a result of this memory you can review the name of the organization that made that toy. Do you see? Our brains are modified to work by relating data, which is likely why psyche maps work so well.

On the off chance that you take a gander at the physiology of the human mind, you would see the focal point of the nerve cell, which branches out to dendrites and axons, etc. Truth be told, this physiological framework has really filled in as the motivation for some, advanced psyche maps. The psyche maps that we see these days are hence intelligent of this and other normal frameworks. Practically all psyche maps are visual. The subjects and subtopics are associated by lines. This makes a progression of data and outwardly shows the connection between subjects.

You need to understand that brain guides and psyche planning are not the equivalent. The demonstration of brain planning is an innovative demonstration which can assist you with sorting out your considerations and plan ahead. The demonstration of psyche planning can help profoundly improve your memory and improve productivity in a significant manner. Brain maps are the final product of psyche planning.

The History of Mind Mapping

The demonstration of brain planning can really be followed back to the third century BC. The Ancient Greeks were the primary known to utilize mind planning for scholarly purposes. Truth be told, the specialized term to portray mind planning, scientific classification, is Greek. There are even references to mind planning and scientific categorizations in the Bible. For example, Adam naming the creatures speaks to a sort of scientific classification.

This sort of ordered arrangement and association of data is in fact a particular sort of psyche map. The idea of brain planning is an overall marvel. Psyche maps have been found to have emerged from Ancient Greece; they were being used all over Europe just as in Asia. Brain maps have been discovered to be interconnected with different religions, the rise of science, and the headways of agribusiness. Think about a genealogical record. A genealogical record isn't actually equivalent to a brain map, however adroitly they are fundamentally the same as.

Previously, mind maps were commonly drawn out by hand. Individuals would regularly utilize circles, triangles, and different shapes to speak to the various levels of data. Bolts and plane lines were, and still are, regularly utilized. These exceptionally plain images were utilized to gather, sort out, and streamline complex data into a visual portrayal, or all the more explicitly a brain map.

Throughout the long term, mind maps have permitted individuals to all the more likely comprehend and review data. As people, we are truly adept at remembering specific sorts of data, particularly visual data. These days, in view of our specialized progressions, assembling a psyche map is unbelievably simple. Today there are many brain planning PC programs accessible, a significant number of which you can get for nothing.

Brain guides will keep on advancing. As people learn and advance mentally, mind maps have gotten progressively valuable. Psyche maps are extraordinary for sorting out numbers, letters, words, thoughts, ideas, etc, so they are probably not going to disappear at any point in the near future. Brain maps are so visual in nature that they permit individuals who are visual scholars to much better grasp the current material just as hold that data. Brain maps are likewise useful to individuals who learn best through discernible or graphical data also since they help individuals to fortify what they have realized.

Extraordinary Mind Mappers in History

Probably the sharpest and most productive individuals in history utilized brain maps normally. This incorporates:

Porphyry of Tyros — This rationalist was one of the first known to utilize mind planning in quite a while educating. This raises a valid statement. In the event that you are an educator who is struggling getting certain things across to your understudies, have a go at utilizing a brain map. Porphyry of Tyros presumably would have disclosed to you the equivalent. He found that he could show others a great deal of data in an a lot speedier way by utilizing this instrument.

Leonardo Da Vinci — This notable verifiable figure carried on with his life in an exceptionally proficient way. He was known to be a painter, creator, engineer, mathematician, essayist, performer, draftsman, botanist, geologist, stone carver, anatomist, and significantly more. Da Vinci utilized psyche maps for note taking. Essentially, he utilized these notes for his very own headways.

Rather than utilizing mind guides to impart ideas and thoughts, he gathered, sorted out, and utilized the data he accumulated from their utilization. Clearly, this permitted Da Vinci to achieve a ton in the course of his life, which is nothing unexpected. Psyche planning permits us to all the more rapidly get our brains around different ideas. It likewise permits individuals to separate substance and rearrange data in various manners for various employments.

Albert Einstein — One of the most extraordinary, if not the most exceptional, personalities of the twentieth century, Albert Einstein was an ardent client of psyche maps. He dismissed numerous sorts of direct, mathematical, and even verbal and made perspectives. He utilized brain maps in numerous whimsical was and he utilized psyche guides to create eccentric perspectives. As indicated by him, this is a piece of where his imaginative virtuoso originated from.

Much like Leonardo Da Vinci, and Galileo before him, Einstein accepted that these kinds of instruments are exceptionally valuable in growing the way that we see the world. He accepted that these kinds of devices were more significant in catching our creative mind than pretty much every other sort of hardware. They likewise permit us to outwardly disclose things to others in a manner that is exceptionally easy to comprehend. At the point when we have content that is composed and organized it is a lot more obvious ourselves and to educate to others. Actually, it pushes and even powers lucidity in deduction.

In particular, Einstein said "Creative mind is a higher priority than information since creative mind is boundless." Not just do mindmaps help you to unfurl your innovative thoughts, yet they help you to bottle them so that you can get it, spread it, show it, share it, and use it. They likewise permit us to develop our perspectives with the goal that we achieve more.

Dr. Allan Collins — Dr. Collins is an American psychological clinician. He is known as one of the dads of current brain planning. Actually, a few people would state that he is the dad of present day mind planning due to his broad responsibility to distributing research about imagination, graphical reasoning and learning, etc. Graphical reasoning is feeling that is both visual and organized. This visual structure doesn't need to be masterful, despite the fact that it is useful when it is. As per Dr. Collins, graphical reasoning can assist us with pushing forward in making more prominent advances, delivering better merchandise and enterprises, and achieving numerical achievements.

Dr. Richard Feynman — Dr. Feynman was an American Nobel Prize winning physicist. At a youthful age he understood that creative mind, imagination, perception, and so forth were the most fundamental in achieving achievements. This is valid. Working with mind guides can help individuals to wipe out issues and explode thoughts. One thing that is unmistakable about brain maps is that they take into consideration more play than different apparatuses. Brain maps are truly adaptable and on the grounds that they are so visual you can mess with them more and use them in an extremely game-like style.

Tony Buzan — Educational expert and current English creator, Tony Buzan, is an energetic backer for mind planning. His conviction is that even proficient and knowledgeable people are limited since that you can't utilize a significant number of the theoretical reasoning instruments that are accessible, including mind maps.

There are numerous different renowned, exceptionally skilled, extremely inventive, and incomprehensibly productive characters in history that pre-owned brain maps consistently, for example, Darwin and Beethoven. Numerous extraordinary chronicled figures additionally had similar perspectives about utilizing mind maps as the absolute most sound researchers of the present day. The imaginative parts of brain planning are regularly what are brought up to be the most significant by these exceptionally keen people.

Facts & Figures about Mind Mapping

Numerous individuals don't realize that Boeing Aircraft was really made from a psyche map. It is currently one of the biggest worldwide makers just as one of the biggest aviation and protection contractual workers on the planet. Considerably all the more intriguing is that psyche map that was use to create Boeing was a stunning 25 feet in length.

Brain planning has been utilized for quite a while. Indeed, even a large number of the old brain guides and others which have been around for a long while stay being used right up 'til today. As should be obvious from the data above, mind maps keep on being helpful in the cutting edge time and that isn't probably going to change at any point in the near future.

Chapter 5: What Are Mind Maps?

"Thanks to Mind Maps you can turn a long and boring list of information into a brilliant, easy to remember and highly organized diagram, your thoughts in tune with the natural processes of your brain." - **Tony Buzan**

Concept

Mind Mapping is an excellent tool that when used for the first time, everything changes from that moment on and it is not discontinued due to its simplicity and because they allow us to retain more easily what we need to understand and improve learning.

A Mind Map is a diagram that synthesizes at a glance, in a logical and creative way, any subject in the educational field or project in the business world. It helps to remember a topic, clarify concepts in a project or memorize information in an orderly and fast way, which is why it is so widely used in these areas.

The creator

Tony Buzan created the concept of Mind Map way back in 1974 when he tried to create a method to facilitate the memorization task, since the texts of endless pages full of sentences became tedious, and made it difficult to understand and remember the information for what he thought on alternative methods to improve this task.

Selecting key words or ideas, changing concepts for representative drawings or symbols, branches to house secondary ideas or concepts, using colours that stimulated the brain, he finally found the method he was looking for, Mind Maps.

We already know that boring, tedious and monotonous things are more easily forgotten than those that catch our attention and images (a picture is worth a thousand words) help to relate concepts and retain said information, favouring learning in a more efficient way efficient.

Main characteristics of a Mind Map

A Mind Map is done around an idea or main word placed in the centre and from which branches are traced that contain words, concepts or secondary ideas and from these in turn, other more concrete, specific or concepts that complement them.

The less relevant, the further away they will be from the main idea, being placed hierarchically on the map. All prepared in a structured, organized and creative way. Words can be represented by images, drawings or symbols and the ramifications drawn with colours that allow ideas to be highlighted, favouring memorization and understanding. Different secondary idea concepts can be connected to each other.

In a schematic way, a Mind Map would be structured like this:

• Canvas: landscape or horizontal sheet where the Mind Map is done.

• Main node: main word or idea.

• Secondary nodes: Secondary concepts linked directly to the main idea, usually radially (although they can have other shapes).

• Ramifications: Unions between a main concept and secondary concepts, as well as these with concepts contained in them of less importance.

• Connections: Associations between concepts of the same branch or a different one.

• Images and drawings: Representations of ideas or concepts.

- Colours: They serve to associate or emphasize certain concepts.

Let's look at a creative example of a Mind Map:

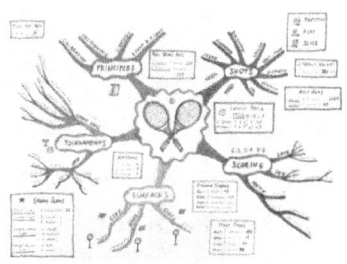

How the human brain learns

The human mind does not learn with monotonous tasks, forced memorization or familiar situations, because there it becomes lazy and ends up forgetting it. However, the new stimuli make lasting learning and memory easier for the brain, such as images, which reach the right hemisphere, creativity and, above all, associating these images with already acquired knowledge.

The brain is not a compendium of independent areas that function in isolation, but is made up of areas, hemispheres, interconnected through neural networks. Emotions are important in learning, which go directly to the amygdala that retains them more effectively, as when they were little, someone burns with a pot in the kitchen and they never forget the consequences, they do not need another bad experience like that to remember, once is enough for a lifetime. And so, with flavours, sounds, images, smells, etc. ... For that reason, the stories that impact us, that move us, always remain recorded and this is a trick for our Mind Maps, using images or photos that cause us such emotion that we will always remember.

The interaction between people, always in a collaborative and cooperative way, stimulates the brain, increasing motivation, creativity and attention, sides that help to better learn concepts and ideas. Mind Maps allow such collaboration, each of the members of a working group contributing ideas.

Chapter 6: Over Recent Years, The Best Mind Mapping Materials.

To beginners Coggle 'Web'.

Mindly for mobile mind mapping 'macOS, iOS, Android'.

Draw.io (Web, Apple, Linux, Android, Chrome OS) is free to use iMindMap for in-depth analysis on your map,iMindMap (Apple, Windows, iOS).

MindMup (Web) for developing MindMeister public mind maps (Web, iOS, Android macOS, Windows) to work on a mind map, with a simple, flexible, non-traditional SmartDraw (Web) mental mapping squad, with Stormboard (Web) for SimpleMind (macOS, Windows, iOS and Android) in-person mind mapping sessions for the development of LucidChart mind maps from PDF (Web, iOS, Android) MindMup (Web).

The best mapping modelling program for beginners is Coggle Web.

As soon as you log in to Coggle, you will see the central node of a new mental map and a fascinating plus sign for adding new nodes and ideas.

When you press the button on the plus sign, Coggle immediately selects the destination of the new node and its orientation to create a new child node.

But maybe you can move the nodes to a size that suits your style a little easier.

You can access keyboard shortcuts by clicking the green question-mark icon in the lower right corner of your canvas if you prefer to use keyboard shortcuts during your mind mapping.

One of our favourite features is that Coggle helps you to arrange your mental map objects and Markdown messages so you can look as sleek as you want when inserting text, photos and connections.

You can go ahead, add any suggestions to your mind map, chat in the sidebar messages and go into full-screen presentation mode to allow a step back and do more high-level thinking.

Pricing Coggle:

optional for up to three individual diagrams; unrestricted $5/month for private layouts and other visualisation resources (like different types and colour controls).

Carefully (macOS, iOS, Android) the best mobile mapping software.

Mind mapping on a mobile device offers a full spectrum of difficulties, due to smaller screen sizes, scrolling and zooming discomfort and readability issues that go along with all of this.

But Mindly's thinking outside the box makes mapping of minds on a phone possible— and, honestly, quite fun.

You will start with your central node, add text and icons, as most mind maps, and change your colour if you want.

Then it's time to add associative thoughts to the next outer layer.

Click every circle you want to add your thoughts to open a new layer immediately and zoom in to work on it.

You also can eventually get back to your first central node by taping the circle at the top left of the screen as you go further into subideas (and into subideas).

Of course, your mobile mind maps can be synchronised with Mindly's desktop version so you can switch from on-the-gogo to a formal mind-mapping session on your desk.

Mindy Price:

Unlimited app mobile contains up to 200 items per mind map; iOS $6.99 with additional features including universal elements, passcode, and search; macOS $29.99.

The best free mind mapping software is Draw.io (Web, macOS, Linux, Windscreen, Chrome OS).

You can draw and create nearly anything you want, including mental maps. Draw.io. With its drag-and-drop canvas, you can add shapes, links, texts and images, change colours, connect your ideas to lines and so on.

Because this is not necessarily an analytical mapping device, you have to work a bit harder to manually add contact lines between concepts and rearrange them to make them fit beautifully on the screen.

However, certain people prefer the lack of models as they allow you a little more freedom to find new, unforeseen connections between concepts.

You may use it straight from your computer as a web-based app, without even signing on to an account. Or, if you prefer to work outside of your browser, go ahead and download the desktop version.

You can note that when you use Draw.io, you endorse a collaboration with Samepage, an app that gives you access to further functionality such as real-time communication and input from team leaders.

If you want the Draw.io free-form mind map design, we recommend the add-on, but we must work on the mind map with other colleagues.

Pricing Draw.io: Free.

The iMindMap software (macOS, Windows, iOS) is the best way to make a thorough analysis of your mental map.

In collaboration with Tony Buzan, who first introduced the accepted practice of mind mapping in the 1960s, the iMindMap software created.

iMindMap provides all you need to build fast and useful mental maps.

The toolbar is a little compelling when you startup with more than two dozen options (including text styles, node styles and more), but all node creation features should click quickly.

Once the basic mental chart is on the board, you can adjust the visual interface with iMindMap.

For example, the time map view can use to provide a more streamlined interface that shows schedules and task lists.

Or you can use a radial map view to naturally break every idea in a series of circular rings and nodes so that correlations between individual designs can be more identify quickly.

iMindMap: $100 for the Home & Student edition with all the basic features of the mind map, $235 for the last version that also provides a radial view of the plan, hierarchical chart display and 3D screen.

The MindMup toolbar is simple to use, offering quick links to all basic needs of mental mapping, from changing the colour of each node to attaching informative texts and attachments to the list.

Nevertheless, it is the freedom to publish and post the mind maps that define MindMup.

MindMup allows you to create and share public mind maps without signing in, while many mind mapping applications need an email address or at least until you are in a place to use their program.

After six months, free spirit maps delete automatically, but if you use it for a fast project, that's the plot while you can always install the Google Drive add-on to enhance your ability to share and work with others.

MindMup Price:

Free for maps of up to 100 kb; for MindMup Gold of $2.99/month, including large plans and partnership.

' MindMeister Pricing:

Unlimited for a basic plan for up to three mental maps and communication in real-time. Just 4,99 $a month for a personal project with free mind maps, file attachments and PDF exports.

collaborative features are wide-ranging:

The purpose of this scheme is that the whole mind chart immediately prevents coordinating the ides, and one definition that invades another never has to be concerned.

The two tools integrated so that you can transform your brainstorm session into an active project, assign individual items on a mind map to your team members, track the progress of the task and synchronise everything with your project boards inside MeisterTask.

For a thorough look at what an example project might look like MindMeister / MeisterTask, take time to read our article entitled "Jumpstart new projects with mind maps.

' MindMeister Pricing: Unlimited for a basic plan for up to three mental maps and communication in real-time. Just 4,99 $a month for a personal project and free mind maps, file attachments and PDF exports.

It is the perfect mind mapping applications for dynamic, non-traditional mind mapping Scapple, Windows.

Most mind maps require you to start with a central node and move from there as new ideas and associations develop your mind. But if you use Scapple, it's more open to seeing where the digital mind map leads.

You're not only launching your mind map with a central theme, for example. Alternatively, you should start with a small idea and then move "backwards" to find the primary purpose.

And Scale lets everything happen organically, as individual nodes only connect when they dragged and dropped on top of each other.

Complex connections can thus quickly drawn up without sacrificing the flow of rapid thinking.

Similar to sure of the other applications on this list, the design of Scapple is relatively straightforward. But this simplicity gives you ultimate flexibility in the way things look and where.

Unless you are in the same physical location, it is not necessary to collaborate in real-time, but you can save the data into your cloud storage so that remote team members can view and update their files.

Prices for Scapple:

$14.99.

SmartDraw Web.

The best linear mind mapping software, SmartDraw will stand out as a right mind mapping solution in a world of curves and circles.

Sub-ideas originate either at the right or the left side of the central node and each sub-idea proceeds in the same direction.

The benefit of this scheme is that the entire mental charts prevent synchronisation of ides immediately and that one concept which invades another should never take into account.

The advantage of such a linear layout does not confine to personality types that prefer straight lines and structures.

It helps the brain to build a metaphysical map with the usual process, then changes gears and explore the meaning of how each thought relates.

SmartDraw Pricing: $9.95/user / month; $5.95/user / month multi-user squad accounts.

Stormboard (Web) Best mind mapping apps in personal mental mapping sessions

Stormboard utilises sticky notes instead of nodes and divisions to monitor the feelings and adjust conventional mental maps.

During the development of the first mind map, you will place the thoughts in different parts of the frame, and incorporate the visual associations with lines afterwards.

Even a "fast fire" mode appears when you post the previous one so you can type your ideas one after another without extra effort— and save the organisation's time for later.

Stormboard often makes it easy to include the entire team, as staff will capture feedback, build assignments and apply their votes to every proposal.

Therefore, you can simplify the cycle with Zapier Integrations from Stormboard and automatically create ideas and storms as events occur in other applications you use most.

Pricing of storm boards:

Personal Free Plan provides a limit of 5 storm boards; from $5 a month, Startup Program providing additional functionality, such as digital logging, Microsoft Office Online live uploading, prototype segment labelling, and other export possibilities.

When you gravitate to build your mind maps with adhesive notes, you may also find Padlet or MURAL.

One of the best mind mapping software for developing mind maps from PDFs (macOS, Mac, iOS, Android) is SimpleMind.

SimpleMind provides a full toolbar with choices, so you don't wonder the apps included, and a range of interface styles (horizontal, vertical, or typically free-form chart style), so that your brainstorming sessions look and feel can be regulated.

When you use SimpleMind on your mobile device, you can add voice and video messages to your mind map, making recording a one-off addition to your mind map easier on the go.

Also, note that you need to keep the data in the cloud instead of locally if you want to use the same mind map through multiple devices.

A unique feature of SimpleMind is that a PDF file can be converted into a mind map automatically. Every time you want to plan the ideas in a book or article, this can save one or more hour of manual work.

When the mind map is to create, you have the freedom to edit and modify it as necessary.

SimpleMind Pricing:

Limited functionality for a free version. Additional features, including uploading images and file sharing included in paid apps.

From $6.99 for mobile applications; apps from desktop start at $24.99 per user (with discounts while buying more licenses).

The most reliable software for transforming the mind map to become an ordered flowchart Web, iOS, is Android.

LucidChart is known primarily as a flowchart technology.

It contains all the elements necessary for creating a mental map, but can also rework and refine your ideas in an organised, detailed flow chart. The development of a mind-map is simple: drag and drop shapes on your mind-map, reflecting any concept and sub-idea.

And create visual connections by clicking and dragging lines between related ideas.

Once you have built a simple mind map, you can use other features of LucidChart to mould your thoughts and fine-tuning connections.

For example, you may decide to enter such details and to automate the next steps in your project, e.g. to create a UML sequence diagram, import CSV files or connect items to Google Sheets data in your plan.

In short, if your mind map needs to turn into something technically more specific, LucidChart gives you the tools to do that.

LucidChart can read files from another like-minded map/ flowchart programs, including Microsoft Visio, Gliffly and Omnigraffle.

LucidChart Pricing:

free of charge for up to three visual chart papers, for the simple scheme of $4.95/month, for infinite shapes and records.

What program should I use?

Mind mapping is an activity of the person what the brain works dictates which technology is better for you.

Typically you are at your office while you're brainstorming, or do you get your best ideas on the road?

Do you think linearly, or do you believe randomly?

Are you tending to brainstorm your team or yourself? Thought about all these issues and used the free trial on all these devices before picking your winner.

The software of the Mind Map is an excellent innovation with many advantages. This dissertation identifies only a few of them.

Mind mapping is an efficient tool. It will open your mind and extend your imagination.

Traditionally mind maps have created with a blank sheet of paper and coded designs.

Just as most people now use the computer to write documents and letters, people also make mind-mapping on the computer.

The benefits of creating a mind map using software rather than conventional paper?

I have listed some of the advantages below.

You will formulate your plans very quickly. You may have a project on which you work or want to function, and you have all these thoughts in your head.

You can use Mind Maps software very quickly to make these ideas very clear and easy to read and analyse.

You won't have to spend hours making coloured lines carefully. These are provided for you automatically.

So you can get these thoughts out of your mind more easily.

It is crucial because one of the suggestions could be a million dollars plan, and you could lose it forever if you do not get it down on paper soon.

After you have passed through a rapid brainstorming session, part of your mind map can rearrange so easily.

It would help if you altered what divisions are linked.

You will move the divisions to other areas of your mind charts. With a traditional pen and paper, this is not possible.

If you've ever created a mind map on a piece of paper, you have run out of space. If you can create a mind map, this is irritating and helps to hinder the cycle of development.

There are no limits to your plan with mind map software.

You can only start, and the program can do it. You can be very creative. You can use just one mind map to plan extensive projects.

Your mind maps will look and feel very professional. All attempts to draw and read handwriting are fantastic.

That's why it is so beautiful to click the printer button and roll off the printer with a thoroughly professional, interactive and vibrant mind map.

After looking at it again and making specific changes, you can print a brand new one that looks fantastic back.

Some mind map program is so sophisticated that you can add photos, website links and shortcuts to documents on your machine to divisions. These are multi-dimensional.

It gives your mind maps a whole new dimension. You will conveniently include relevant links and records in your maps of mind. Also, conventional pen and ink actually can not be used.

It makes it much more enjoyable to use the machine. Mind mapping helps you think as the mind likes to think. It's swift and imaginative. It helps to expand your thoughts.

You will be pleased about using your device with mind map apps. You 'll begin to chart all kinds of things you're involved therein.

All of these topics would prove to be much stronger and more informative.

Chapter 7: Building Mind Maps The Right Way

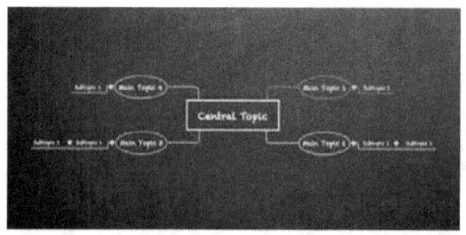

Brainstorming and mind mapping are not the same and are not an interchangeable concept, but they could be used together to obtain common goals such as problem solving, focusing research and developing structure for a project or any large chunk of information.

First, mind mapping is thinking, planning and a note taking tool that can be used in many different contexts, not only with brainstorming. Next, brainstorming can be conducted with many different office products such as post-it notes, flip-charts, 3x5 index cards or mind maps.

Brainstorming - Brainstorming is intended to expand your thinking on a particular topic or subject and is often done in groups or meetings and as part of a team or as an exercise to build upon one another's ideas.

Mind Mapping - Mind mapping can then be used to organize the outcome of the brainstorming session and help realize the relationships between ideas and different content.

The two-stage process consists of stage-one: free thinking and stage-two: organizing stage. These two stages should be done in this order and never mixed together for best results.

Stage-One

Brainstorming = Free Thinking + Producing Ideas

Using a blank piece of paper, write your problem or topic in the center.

Start with colored pencils and markers and free association. Write and draw anywhere on the paper about anything that comes to mind regarding or related to the topic in the center. Do not edit or filter yourself or go back and cross out or erase anything on the paper, just allow your thoughts and ideas to flow, no matter how bad or outrageous you think they might be.

Stage-Two

Mind Mapping = Identifying Relationships + Organizing Ideas

Using words, arrows and lines in various colors, identify and link the relationship between the key points and ideas on your brainstorming paper to create a mind map.

When you have completed the second step, you can begin to look at your mind map to find similarities and contrasts and cause and effect to help you solve a problem, focus your research or organize the ideas and notes you've just mapped out.

Mind Mapping, the Analogy Method

The analogy method is basically shifting ideas, concepts and thoughts from other areas to help locate a solution to a problem.

1 - On a sheet of paper, formulate two branches that will serve as the main areas. Label one "Ideas" and the other "Concept Area"

2 - Under the Concept Area, add a sub-branch with a larger space for topics you are reasonably knowledgeable in. These topics could be anything from "knot tying" or "toy ship building" to "accounting". The topics do not have to be related to the field or profession of your problem.

3 - For each of the topic areas chosen in Step 2, list several major concepts relating to that area. For the knot tying area, you might write "Figure-of-eight", "Overhand

knot", "Double fisherman's knot", "Strangle knot" and so on.

4 - It is now time to relocate ideas from Step 3 to your problem. If your problem was an issue with creating costumes for a play, you could use some of the knot tying list to come up with creative ideas to solve the issue. For example, if one set of costumes needed to be switched on-stage from a man's suit to a woman's long skirt; you might find the solution in the "Overhand knot".

Chapter 8: Mind Maps – An Overview

Mind maps are very powerful tools to help you creatively solve problems, remember better, map out ideas and plans and to take action. Mind maps encourage you to be creative and flexible and assist you to think outside of the box.

Invented by Tony Buzan, mind maps have proven to be highly effective and have become extremely popular with both the self-help community and students of management theory.

Because mind maps allow you to create a visual representation of a book, seminar, concept, etc. they really help you to remember facts and details. Most people are conditioned to respond to visual stimuli (mainly from a familiarity with television and movies) and so respond very well to a mind map.

Mind maps help you to stop thinking in a linear fashion and open you up to creative, new ways of thinking. They allow you to realistically represent ideas, concepts and details in a concise and clear manner, because most of nature is chaotic and un-ordered in the first place.

A mind map is a useful tool to help you get the bigger picture and naturally tap in to the creativity and intuition that resides in the right hand side of your brain.

Those people that use and understand mind maps become raving fans of them because they realise just how helpful and useful they are. Students who use mind maps to help them study for exams report greater recall of facts and improved connecting together of information. They also report that mind maps assist in learning subjects and recalling information from textbooks.

Managers who use mind maps find themselves to be more relaxed and stress free because they are organized. They are also known for creative thinking and problem solving.

Creating a mind map is a fun process that really unleashes the creativity inside of you. You can create a mind map on a computer using specialist mind-mapping software, or you can use your word processor or other software to create your own mind maps.

However, many people prefer to create mind maps by hand, on paper, because it can encourage creativity and allows them to easily see the bigger picture. You'll need a piece of paper, turned on its side in landscape format, to produce the best mind maps.

The advantage of a computer program though, is that you can layer your mind maps and it is very easy to make changes without messing up your diagram with scribbles and crossing out.

Mind maps are powerful tools that everyone can use in their lives. Learning to use mind maps will help make studying easier, recollection of facts faster and unlock the more creative part of your mind.

Chapter 9: How To Personalize A Mind Map

While I have only covered the bare minimum in the last chapter, I hope you don't get the impression that there is not much to the technique of Mind Mapping. It's not like that. You can come up with hundreds and thousands of ways to draw a same Mind Map with the same entries, and each version will have a different effect on you. That is why Mind Map can be used for both of two seemingly opposite purposes: creative thinking, which is unrestricted in nature and can be categorized as the so-called "right brain" activity; and organized and analytical thinking, which is more focused and a "left brain" activity[1]Now that you know how to draw a Mind Map and hopefully using it in your daily life, let's discuss ways you can experiment with the various elements of Mind Map.

Color

Mind Map is a visual technique, and color is a vital part of your visual senses. While black-and-white Mind Map is much more effective than traditional linear note taking, using colors on a Mind Map opens up a whole new set of possibilities. You can use different colors for each subtopic, or use the colors as a means to highlight particular entries. If there is a pre-established association between a keyword and a color (such as carrot-orange, elephant-gray, or even Democratic party-blue) it can make the connections within your brain that much firmer.

Size

Size is another notable visual element. You can write the keywords that are closer to the central topic bigger to represent the hierarchy, or emphasize a particular word by writing it bigger than other words on the same level. In addition to the words themselves, you can change the thickness of the lines. While some people might find using a uniform weight on all the lines more effective, others might prefer starting out thick, then thinning out as it goes further away from the center, just like the branches do in nature.

Figure 3-1. Example of Mind Map with fairly uniform keyword size and line weight

Figure 3-2. Example of Mind Map with varied keyword sizes and weight

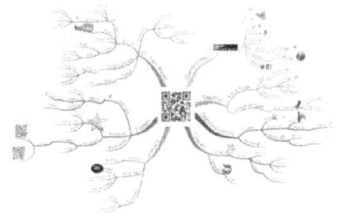

Shapes

You can also use different shapes such as circles, ovals, and rectangles to categorize the concepts or emphasize some over the others. Think about how a flow chart is drawn: it uses different shapes to represent different types of actions (start & finish, action and decision). Shapes are a great way to further organize your thoughts along with color and size.

Lines or shapes?

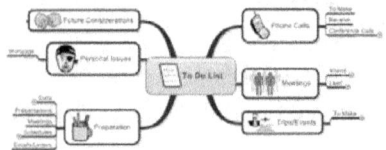

There are two ways to write the keywords. One is to write them on a line, therefore making the lines continuous as it stems from the central keyword. The other is to write them in a shape or just in an empty space without the lines. Here is an example that shows the two alternatives on one map:

Figure 3-3. Keywords can be written in a shape or on a line.

I think this falls in the category of personal preference. While Tony Buzan claims that keywords should be written on a line, I personally prefer a simple circle, a thin line so that it doesn't interfere the keyword visually, or nothing at all around the keywords. Or you can even use a hybrid form of these two. You can write a keyword in a shape, along with some annotations as necessary above the connecting line, like the concept maps I briefly described in Chapter 1. Whichever way you choose, I advise you to be creative with the process itself and devise new effective ways to organize and represent your thoughts.

Symbol

Here is where the fun begins. Only humans possess the ability to take something as a representation of something else; that is, to use symbols. The words and language used in Mind Maps are a type of symbols too. Since Mind Map triggers your brain to tap into more intuitive functions, symbols are not only a fun twist to your Mind Map but also can be a powerful creativity booster. Start with standard symbols such as the question mark or plus sign, then venture into coming up with your own. If you integrate Mind Map into your everyday life (which I strongly recommend you do), you will find it handy if you can replace some of the recurring concepts or ideas with symbols.

Images

Another fun way to tweak the Mind Map, you can draw or paste an image to represent a concept. If you are doing a hand-drawn Mind Map and you have decent drawing skills, you'll find this enjoyable and visually stimulating for your brain. If you can't draw, don't worry.

There are computer-based software programs which provide you with a lot of clip-art samples so you don't have to do it yourself. **Chapter 5** will give you a more comprehensive review of computer-based Mind Mapping. Regardless of the method you use, this is a great way to make the Mind Map more "alive" and effective.

Different line shapes

In addition to the thickness that I mentioned earlier, you can experiment with different shapes of the connecting lines. You can make it shorter or longer, straight or curved, the space between them wider or narrower, all depending on the significance of each particular concept or the purpose of your Mind Map. In other words, you might find using straight lines with standard print when organizing a course material for a test, while you might find it more interesting to use curvy lines and funny fonts when you are brainstorming for your short story.

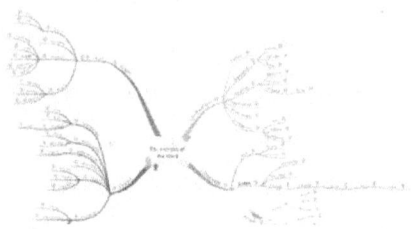

Figure 3-4. Example of free-form Mind Map

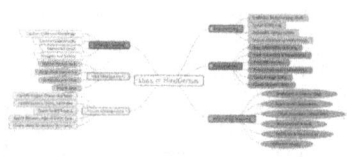

Figure 3-5. Example of "organized" Mind Map

Overall layout of the Mind Map

Combining all the elements (and more, if you can think of other ways) of customization discussed so far, it will be beneficial for you if you can think of the overall layout of the Mind Map and how you will make it fit the purpose for which you are drawing it. As mentioned earlier, if you are trying to organize lecture notes and turn them into a Mind Map which explains the course material thoroughly yet concisely, you might want to make it neat and tidy, with little oddities if any. However, if you are making a presentation and trying to use the Mind Map as a powerful and convincing communication tool, you will want to use some colors along with appropriate symbols and images. Furthermore, in this case, you will experiment with various different arrangements of the ideas in trying to figure out the best and most convincing option; while most of the times you will use the simple chronological order in the case of the lecture notes.

The whole point here is to see what works best for you and what you are trying to achieve. The former is about figuring out the personal propensities and leveraging them to maximize the effectiveness of the Mind Map for you. The latter is about the purpose of the Mind Map and the specific usage of the Mind Map for a specific occasion. The personal preferences you need to do the experimentation yourself. For the purposes, I'll elaborate on them and cover some of the best uses of a Mind Map in the next chapter. As you read along, not only will you notice that the possibilities for Mind Map are almost limitless, but also start to think about what style of Mind Mapping would be best for each use. Also, you can find some examples of Mind Maps done in different styles in the **Appendix**. You'll see how the elements discussed in this chapter pans out in the real-life examples.

Chapter 10: The Correct Way To Make A Mind Map

There are a lot of different ways you could make a mind map, but there is a defined set of symbols and a process for creating a mind map which, if you follow, makes the mind map easier for you to understand and something other people can understand.

Before you start, you will need some pens and pencils. If you have some colored ones, then that will help. These can easily be picked up at a local store for a few dollars. You will also need some paper; the paper needs to be in landscape format (i.e., the longest edge is at the top). This gives you more typical space to draw your mind map in.

In the center of the piece of paper, you want to write the main concept that you are mind-mapping about. This needs to be in the center so that everything else can relate to it and radiate out from this central point. This visual method is very helpful in assisting you to remember and understand the core concepts.

If you are mind-mapping a seminar, book, or revision, then you will write out your mind map as you go along and learn. If you are mind-mapping to solve a problem, then your mind map will be much more free-form, and you will need to write it out without allowing your conscious mind to interfere too much. You draw the mind map without stopping until you have it all down.

You can be as creative as you want with your mind map. Some people prefer to use boxes and words, whereas others like to use colors and pictures for their mind map. This is a personal preference and depends upon what works best for you. If the former is best for you, then use that, but if you prefer the latter, then use that. There is no right or wrong answer; it's a personal preference.

Often an image can work much better because a picture is truly worth a thousand words and opens up your creativity and other associations. Using color here is a good idea too because it stimulates your brain and grabs your attention. Make sure your picture is a good size because you need to be able to see it clearly and have enough room to join other concepts on to it.

Around this central image, you need to put the main points you want to cover. These are words that need to be in capital letters as they are very important. They are like the chapters of a book. Connect these to the central image using bold (or colored) curved links, like a branch to the trunk of a tree.

Printing these concepts in capital letters helps the brain to photograph the words, which allows you to recall it better. Try to use just a single word if you can, as it's easier for the brain to memorize that. If you do use more than one word, do not split it on to separate lines because the line break will disconnect the words in your brain.

If you use curved lines to join these words to the central image, this gives a visual rhythm to the diagram, making it easier to remember and is more pleasing on the eye. By making these lines thicker, you are denoting them as being more important, which again, is noted in the brain.

Next, you add a second level to each branch. These are again words or images that trigger concepts or information. The words are still printed, but you can use lower case rather than joined-up writing. Make the connecting lines thinner because they are further from the center.

Don't worry about finishing one branch before moving on to the next; you are allowing the information to flow naturally.

The smaller words and the smaller lines denote that these are further from the center and less important.

You can then add a third and even fourth level of information as you see fit. Again, using images is very helpful because these can convey large amounts of information in a small area. If you are artistically challenged, then you can print out or cut out pictures if necessary.

At these levels, allow your brain to jump around as necessary, recording the information that you need to recall later on.

For some of the key points, you may want to add boxes around certain words and images to draw your attention to these points and help you to memorize them.

You may want to draw a colored box around a branch of your mind map, with the box tight to the branch. These outlines can create shapes that your mind can interpret as clouds and help you to remember the concepts. You can use the same colors on different branches to show there is a connection between the branches.

Mind maps are meant to be fun to build, so enjoy the process of making one and get creative. The more you personalize your mind map and make it your own, the more powerful and effective it will be for you.

Below you can see a small mind map based on words and get fit:

When you draw out your mind map, you can expand this, use colors, pictures, and more to make a mind map that not only appeals to you but also actually works for you.

Using Colors, Shapes, and Symbols

The use of colors in your mind map can help you to remember the information that you are mind-mapping. Which colors you use is very much down to personal preference, but there are some colors that almost universally relate to certain concepts:

Green—this signifies go. Think about traffic lights here. You can use green to signify action points.

Red—often it means stop, so it can be used for problems or concerns.

Yellow—it can be used for caution or for items that need to be thought about.

Remember that whatever color scheme you choose to use, you need to be consistent throughout your mind maps; otherwise, it is going to get very confusing very quickly.

You can use shapes for the concepts in your mind map. The recommended shapes vary from expert to expert and between different software programs. Whichever you decide you are going to use, you need to make sure you are consistent in your mind maps.

The main idea at the center of your page is often illustrated with a circle or oval. If you are using an image, then you can draw a circle or oval around the picture.

You could use a star shape for action points or things to think about. A rectangle can make a good shape to put around your second and third level concepts. You could use a triangle for concern or problem (remember that many warning road signs are triangles).

If you are using software, then you will find that each piece of software will have its own recommended shapes, which can vary.

When drawing a mind map, a lot of people use standard flow chart symbols because it is something that many people learn at school and are familiar with. If you want to use these, then that could work very well for you.

Whatever colors, shapes, and symbols you decide you are going to use in your mind map, remember that you need to be consistent with them across your mind maps. If you do not remain consistent, then you may find that your mind maps become confusing and lose their ability to help you remember things.

Color and shapes are a very powerful way for you to enhance the effectiveness of a mind map. Use them well, and you can find your mind maps become easier to remember and far more effective more you.

Studying and Note-Taking with Mind Maps

Mind maps are excellent tools to help you with your studying and also with note-taking from seminars, meetings, or books. Because they engage your whole brain and unleash your creativity, they help you to remember and organize facts and data. You can recall vast amounts of information just from looking at your mind map.

When creating a mind map for studying and note-taking, you to need to have multiple mind maps (or layers in a software program) for the subject, a single mind map would take up a very large piece of paper.

If you start with a single sheet of paper and have the main subject in the middle and then draw your mind map out for the top level subjects and notes, then you create additional mind maps on separate pieces of paper for each topic within the main subject. If you are using software to create your mind map then you can layer your mind maps in some of the tools provided; otherwise, just linking together pieces of paper can work.

Some people though prefer to buy a large sheet of paper and create one big mind map. Whether you choose this or separate pieces of paper is entirely up to you and depends on what you feel more comfortable with.

If you are using a mind map to take notes then you may want to create a mind map for each chapter of a book, for example, and then a higher-level mind map to encompass all of the concepts and information within the book.

Mind-mapping for studying and note-taking is done in the same way as a normal mind map, except you may want to include a little bit more information on it. You don't want to write out lots and lots of info on your mind map, but you do want enough for you to recall the information whilst taking care not to add so much that you get overwhelmed.

So if you were mind-mapping to take notes on the Olympics you might produce something like this:

You can see that the main topic is in the middle and then there are the chapter headings surrounding this and then more detail on each one.

The key here is that each of the points captures something in a few words. When you read "New Stadium Built" above it reminds you of the Olympic complex that was built and you can have other facts about this too.

"Held in East London" triggers other information, like it was held in Stratford in East London, and then it follows on with more information.

Some people prefer to write out notes by hand and then draw a mind map from the notes. They can then refer to the notes as well as the mind map.

Using a mind map is a great aid to studying, and you will find that it helps you to encapsulate information very concisely. By glancing at your mind map, you can very quickly recall large amounts of information because the mind map triggers the release of information in your brain.

Using pictures rather than words can be extremely effective when using a mind map to help you study. Most people who use mind maps whilst studying report that they find it easier to organize and recall information plus they mentally are less stressed about their studying. "Mind mappers" find their exams are easier because they can easily recall the information and can relate the facts to each other, allowing them to answer questions well.

Chapter 11: Mind Map Creating Techniques

Pen and Paper

Most, if not all, individuals who engage in mind mapping probably did so with pen and paper first. There are some tremendously elaborate mind mapping software programs available for your PC, laptop and even your smartphone. However, there are some individuals who feel like nothing beats the mind-body connection of pen and paper when trying to solve a problem or amp up their creativity.

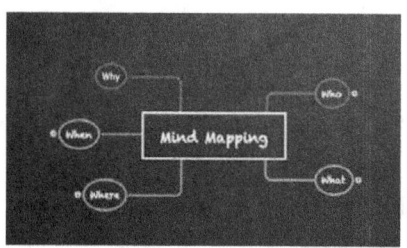

Advantages of Pen and Paper Mind Mapping

There is a multitude of benefits for constructing hand-drawn mind maps just as there are advantages to using computer software programs. This list is for the benefits of using pen and paper to make mind maps and not a comparison to software programs for mind mapping.

Portability - Using pen and paper for mind maps lend itself to portability as they can be constructed whenever and wherever you are. Because ideas and "things to do" come to you at all hours, and not always at the most convenient times, you are able to capture them quickly.

Pencils, pens and paper go almost anywhere and a mind map can be created on just about anything; it does not have to be paper. Experiment creating mind maps on canvas, rolls of paper, flipcharts, wipeboards and blackboards or even blank walls, the limit is only your imagination.

Notable - Once you start making mind maps using pen and paper, you will find they are highly addictive. Creating mind maps will reveal your unknown brainpower, experiences and understanding to help you learn new things. Because you are using pen and paper, a physical act, it becomes notable, memorable and meaningful while at the same time helping you to discover and cultivate your creativity as well as clarify your thinking. Since the images and text has been created in your own handwriting, they will assist in your recall.

Style - Evolving into your own style is something that will take a little time and practice, but is also fun as it emerges from those first mind maps. Drawing ability and style are going to be as individual as the person creating the mind map; no two are going to be similar. The versatility and flexibility are yours to create a mind map that twists and turns, is flamboyant and flashy or simple and orderly or soft or edgy.

Distinctive - As you hand-draw more mind maps, your personal style emerges. Almost like an artist with their trademark signature and identifiable marks, your mind maps will be distinctive in color, style and look. Do not make a fuss over what you think might be mistakes, because they become part of the landscape and may even become part of the solution or process for what you are mapping out.

Direct - The physical act of formulating a mind map is instantaneous and progressive; immediately, you have direct flow from your brain to the paper where you capture your ideas and thoughts before you can forget them. Hand-drawn inspires thinking, emotions and feelings from your body and all senses to help ignite your creativity mixed with reasoning to capture your individuality before you on the paper.

Mind mapping by hand-drawing is fun and combines the physical, emotional, mental, tactile, intimate and personal elements. Its flexibility taps into every part of your brainpower as well as your senses, which then works together to travel the path the map has laid out.

Computer

As with all things since the beginning of time, mind mapping has changed, grown and evolved. Technology has created advancements in software that allows mind mapping on your desktop PC, laptop, tablet and smartphone. And similar to those who would rather create their mind map using pen and paper, there are an equal number of individuals who would rather use a specific software program for their mind mapping project.

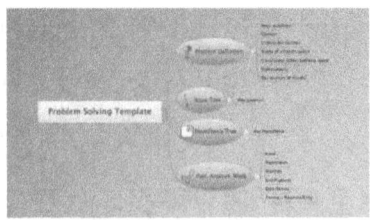

Advantages of Mind Mapping Software

There are many benefits for using mind mapping software. Business professionals, teachers, students and individuals who want to become more organized, creative or solve a problem in their personal life could do so with the assistance of software specifically designed for mind mapping.

Embedding - Many mind mapping software programs allow the user to embed links, documents, data and notes within the structure of your map to convert it into what is equal to a commanding visual file. This translates to a task or assignment map with short-cuts as much supportive information to back-up your project when needed. For the most part, it will not matter if your mind map is sorted as an Excel spreadsheet, individual email, Word document or web pages, all the information and data pertaining to this particular project or assignment will be linked within the main mind map and only a mouse click away.

Storage - Mind mapping software allows for collapsible and expandable topic trees to add to the storage space for information. This permits larger jobs to be sub-divided into a more manageable and controllable design.

Collaboration - There are mind mapping software programs designed for collaborative purposes. The completed mind maps can be uploaded to office sharing workstations, emailed to clients, vendors or others who need to view the final map or team members who could work on the mind map further or add annotates. Some of the mind mapping software applications allow for many individuals to work on the same map at one time.

Versatile - Be its very nature, mind mapping software for computers are versatile and flexible because you can re-arrange, delete and change topics, paths, lines, colors, graphics, pictures or anything and everything easily and quickly. Some of the mind mapping software will allow you to track or save your modifications in case you change your mind and want to go back to your original context.

Sharing - One of the major benefits of mind mapping software is it allows you to share with an audience such as in a meeting or presentation style setting, but in better, more advanced ways than PowerPoint. If you have a Q & A after your presentation of your mind map at the end, you can put your client's questions, answers and suggestions directly into the mind map, updating it in real time, which could increase their interest in your idea.

Mind mapping using computer software applications can be advantages on many levels, for big and small businesses with a large number of employees or only a few employees. If integration from other software applications and technology is needed, then mind mapping software may be the right type of mind map tool for you.

Chapter 12: Mind Mapping In Business

A brain map is essentially a diagram used to organize data, designed to help companies enhance brainstorming sessions, in addition to cooperation and communication.

A mind map may be used by companies to emphasise notions and thoughts . By copying ideas to a diagram, it is possible to turn frequently complex, dull data into an organized, vibrant and memorable centered format.

You will find hordes of brain mapping tools available to small companies, designed to boost job collaboration, cooperation, clarity and efficacy.

By visualizing thoughts, theories and advice, mind maps help individuals follow discussions and lead meetings economically and effectively.

Mind mapping is being used as a substitute for more conventional methods of presenting, like using flip charts or PowerPoint.

#increase productivity

By enabling the free flow of thoughts in a controlled fashion and producing simple visualization, brain mapping can reduce the completion time of unique jobs, thus significantly boosting a group's productivity. Firms use the tool for conferences, meetings, preparation and more, resulting in greater productivity with an average 25%.

Many advocates also assert that 20 hours of work can be achieved in only six hours by simply using a mind mapping program.

#enhance meetings

Also as increased productivity, using mind mapping may be an important instrument in improving encounters. For instance, brain mapping reveals key words and significant points immediately, meaning meeting participants are not as likely to overlook anything.

This visual sort of presenting helps other folks imagine, which may enhance memory, meaning participants are more inclined to remember significant points raised at a meeting.

#optimize project management

From organizing multiple, frequently distant teams, maintaining together with workflows, and ensuring each portion of a job is handled so deadlines are met, and goods are completed in time, job management basically deals with organized chaos.

Mind mapping could be utilized to simplify tasks and make easy to-do lists. Advanced brain mapping tools empower users to insert particular task info, making job management simpler and much more efficient.

From 'professional doodling' that empowers employees to discuss and present strategies using a vibrant, visualized diagram, to work delegation by which a whole map or maybe just a couple of branches signify which group members are responsible for different jobs, to brainstorming sessions and used as a note-taking tool, brain mapping software is an invaluable tool in assisting small companies to get organized via optimized job administration.

#improve collaboration and communication

Collaboration and communication can also be improved through brain mapping. Using online tools may be a good way for groups to collaborate, share and communicate ideas and theories, especially for groups that operate remotely from various places.

#mind mapping for creative thinking and innovation

Creative thinking and innovation are just two of the most significant prerequisites for continuing small business achievement. With spatial designs and picture and icon libraries, creating a brain map is a powerful way for companies to think of creative, innovative techniques to emphasise a problem, produce a marketing effort, create a new solution, or make a pitch.

By changing substantial lists of frequently dull and elaborate information into an extremely coordinated, memorable, and vibrant pictorial representations, mind maps help stimulate ideas and foster innovation and creativity within a little company.

Mind mapping isn't hard to get companies to master. As soon as they have, this kind of visual outlining provides a strong tool to create increased business, efficiency, productivity, creativity and innovation.

Within the last few years, head mapping has been acknowledged by firms as a powerful communication tool that enhances counselling and collaboration sessions. By imagining concepts and relations, folks may follow discussions better and lead more during encounters. Mind mapping can be regarded as an option to conventional linear presentations like PowerPoint or other charts.

Boost productivity

Boost meetings

Simplify ask for proposals (rfp)

Review understanding management

Optimize project direction

Improve cooperation and communication

#mind mapping productivity boost

Professional mind mapping applications like mindview, mindgenius and mindmanager comprise integration with ms office, allowing users to move thoughts maps to other files like word summaries or PowerPoint presentations. These export options guarantee ROI for brain mapping users, as there are not any requirements to re-enter any info, instead of classic whiteboard or other chart sessions.

Mind mapping and project management

When it comes to project management, brain mapping can be used to make easy to-do lists or much more complicated work breakdown structures (wbs). A few of the more innovative brain mapping tools enable you to insert activity information on roll and branches off this info, thereby creating these applications perfect for visualizing jobs or developing a wbs. A number of brain mapping programs also have an integrated Gantt graph or ms project integration, allowing users to move the work breakdown structure to a Gantt graph without re-entering data.

Collaboration online through mind mapping

Visualizing mind maps within an internet environment is a potent approach to collaborate and improve staff work, particularly when working from other locations. It's also a wonderful way to present ideas and concepts to prospective customers. Online mind mapping applications or desktop mapping applications with shared workspace integration provides customers with a cloud-based platform and applications that allow for multiuser editing in real time, which makes multi-regional teams more successful across the business.

Ways to use mind maps at business

#present

Present something distinct and deliver with effect. Head maps permit you to brainstorm ideas, create a plan of action, and introduce it to your coworkers all in one area. By using keywords, mind maps promote better, more succinct and more stimulating demonstrations. The mix of key words along with the visually stimulating structure of a mind map is demonstrated to boost recall of data and permit you to take care of hard puzzles with confidence. Imindmap's display mode delivers a refreshing alternative to presenting slides, providing you with a highly visual and productive means of distributing your message. You are able to attach documents, webpages, sound clips as well as PowerPoint slides into the branches inside imindmap, making a truly multimedia demonstration, readily manipulated from inside your mind map.

#plan

Plan your programs, meetings, briefs and suggestions in a new and more efficient manner of mind maps. It's possible to divide up issues and tasks into various branches, including sub-topics and smaller, more related jobs as kid branches. Then it's possible to draw links between related jobs, see how distinct endeavors impact one another and prioritise you to do so. Create 'to do' lists, plan your weekly schedule, build a 3-month advertising plan or establish goals for your year. A mind map is the best area to organise and set data in a transparent and coherent manner -- cover all facets in one spot, from aims and goals, to sources and places, which means you can stay organized and on the ball.

#consolidate

Using a mind map, you can combine a huge array of data, and with the imindmap software, you'll be able to take this into a multimedia degree with whatever, from spreadsheets to sites to sound files. Considering all the pertinent information at your fingertips, all in one mind map, you're in command and can save hours of time. You can throw all the links and documents concerning a particular project you are working on, attaching documents into the appropriate division of your job map. You've got total control in imindmap along with the capacity to produce your own library of information that's easily navigated and on a single screen. Adding new info or amending present data is straightforward as you are not tied into a rigid arrangement -- a mind map is a living document.

project manage

Project management

Handle time, resources and data to attain new levels of productivity using imindmap's award winning project management system. Create mind maps to scope projects, then add dates, tasks, predecessors, landmarks and durations. Incorporating Gantt graphs, task tables and mind maps, this instrument could be completely integrated with outlook and Microsoft projects to guarantee you never leave a job unfinished or late again.

problem solve

Locate innovative solutions with a tool that offers a space for investigating connections between the numerous aspects of an issue and arouses creative and critical thinking. By making a mind map, you can see all the components of an issue at once -- sparking creative integration and association. The procedure acts as a trigger device for your own imagination and motivates your mind to monitor thoughts that usually lie in obscurity in the border of your believing. The imindmap software provides you total freedom to control and draw links between your thoughts, without interrupting your train of thought. If you have ever felt as though you're hitting your head against a brick wall trying to find a remedy or think of a new concept, you have to attempt mind mapping!

#collaborate

Collaborate with others to develop plans or execute key jobs. A mind map permits you to exploit the input of members of a team in a lively and creative manner and is demonstrated to boost critical thinking. Contributions could be added to the relevant branches and explored further or placed on hold for later debate. Together with imindmap, you could even capture sound notes and attach them to a map to guarantee no remark is missed without sacrificing the momentum of this dialogue.

#see the larger picture

A mind map is a perfect platform for bettering your business, making conclusions and anticipating potential dangers. Pest, swot, five forces, smart, six thinking hats, four p's, balanced scorecard, value chain analysis and other business versions you might desire to research may be simplified and improved by utilizing a mind map as your own workspace. The radiating character of a mind map lets infinite growth of thoughts whilst maintaining a coherent and organized structure -- supplying you with the entire image in one visual photo.

CHAPTER 13: CREATIVITY BRINGING OUT THE BEST IN YOU

In this chapter, we are going to discuss about creativity and it is important in idea mapping because the process itself encourages your creativity to be used in producing ideas and key points related to your main topic. In addition to that, creativity is also very important in the writing process itself and so here are tips on how to make use of your creativity in doing an idea map:

Add colors. Our mind wants to process something creative and adding different colors to your lines and boxes in our idea maps not only makes it interesting but also, easier to remember making it memorable and retain in our brain. The idea map is very important in the writing process because it creates the structure of your writing that can prevent the writer's block.

Use symbols or images. Aside from adding colors, make use of symbols or images in your key point or chapters. It works the same way as adding colors, making your idea more interesting, fun, and more importantly, memorable and easy to remember.

Aside from learning how to use creativity in your idea mapping, it is important to remember that sometimes, creativity is just not there and sometimes, not enough to allow you to make good idea maps and writings. In addition to that, creativity is not something that's innate, it is developed and it needs to be improved so here are some ways on how you can increase your creativity for a better idea mapping and writing:

Listen to classics. When you want to boost your creativity, research says that listening to classical music can actually stimulate and increase your creativity. So download those Mozart masterpieces and listen while you write.

Doodle. You know when you are in a class lecture and you just don't want to focus on it and you doodle your life away from all the uninteresting lessons? Most students get scolded when actually not paying attention to class lectures and when they just doodle during it. But this time, doodling is just what you need. Research says that doodling increases creativity and stimulates our brain so we can produce new ideas. So in the case of writing, bring your paper out and start doodling prior to idea mapping so you can max out your creativity just in time for idea mapping and writing.

Go out of your comfort zone and do something you have never done. Creativity gets a big boost when you leave your comfort zone and actually do something new. Try taking up classes you have always wanted to. If you are a frustrated dancer, why not sign up for a beginner's class and start learning. As they say, better late than never. And in the case of idea mapping and writing, doing this will be a good investment because you not only satisfy your hunger for more learning in what you have always wanted to do, you also boost your creativity that you will be needing for idea mapping and writing.

Modify your working space. As they say in science classes, life flourishes when the right environment is there and so does creativity! Adjust your working space, maybe your desk and your room and turn them into the perfect environment for your creativity to thrive in. When you are in a comfortable and relaxed environment for creativity to happen, you can start doing an awesome idea map and writing.

Do the 30 circles activity. This particular activity stimulates your mind to be creative and it is done by drawing 30 circles in a piece of paper and in a minute or two, you have to be able to associate and turn these circles into things you can imagine. Turn it into a wheel, a mask, or maybe even a whole pizza. This will encourage you to be more creative and will definitely help you deal with your idea map and writings.

Start and daydream. Research shows that daydreaming increases your creativity but only after you have started with what you are doing. Since we are discussing on idea mapping, start doing it and then allow yourself to daydream and visualize your thoughts. It is like allowing your ideas to grow and multiply while you are there sitting in your office chair staring at the wall clock.

Think about your audience. We have mentioned in the past chapter to know your audience in order to adjust to their needs and get successful with your idea map and writing but in the case of creativity, simply thinking that someone out there will be reading your masterpiece can encourage more creativity in you. So, do not forget about your readers as you do your idea map and writings!

Put a little pressure on yourself. We have told you to create a comfortable and relaxed environment to increase creativity but too much of it can make you feel complacent and not really be creative. So why not put a little pressure, let's say set a time for you to accomplish something. When you feel a little pressure, you also boost creativity by thinking that you have to come up with something given this certain amount of time.

Have optimism. Motivate yourself by thinking of the good memories you had with your best friends. Reminisce and think back on things you laughed about. Visualize your goals and imagine yourself actually succeeding on what you are doing which is coming up with a good idea map and writing.

Look at greens and blues. Research shows that the color green and blue boosts your creativity. Blue can be associated with sea and sky symbolizing openness while green can be associated with plants and trees symbolizing growth.

Talk to your people. When we are with friends we are comfortable with, we open our hearts to them and creativity flourishes. So go ahead and catch up with your loved ones and closest of friends and have your deep talks that have long been overdue.

Chapter 14: Getting Started

The basic principles of mind mapping

The principles of mind mapping have been around for thousands of years, however most people are unaware of its true power. Often times, even people who do use mind mapping are not using it to its full potential.

Putting your thoughts on paper in a way that represents an organized structure allows you to visualize the necessary steps to complete a project or achieve a goal. Linear list making and note taking tend to produce linear thoughts and ideas. Mind mapping treats all ideas equally.

When you create a mind map, though, it allows the mind to recall key words and images far more easily than sentences. In fact, an entire mind map is easier to recall than one page of traditional notes. It is a non-linear way to organize the information, and it is a technique that allows you to capture the natural course of your ideas. By using it, you will be able to see things from different perspectives!

Mind mapping is a free flowing process. For this reason, there are no right or wrong ways to do it. Instead, there are helpful suggestions and guides (like what you will see in this book) that can make the process easier for you. Nothing is off limits when it comes to your own creativity and thoughts.

If you are creative or a visual learner, you can use colored pencils and images or symbols in your mind map. If not, words will do just fine. The most important thing is to just get started, and you can perfect your methodology as you go along.

A great visual for better understanding a mind map is to think of map of a city. The center of the city represents the MAIN IDEA, while the main streets that connect the center with the rest of the city are key ideas that emerge from the process of thinking and developing ideas.

The small lines that connect to the major components, also called twigs or branches, represent the minor characteristics, or components of lesser importance. As you can see, the mind map creates a visual representation of the major and minor components of the topic.

It doesn't need to be extravagant to be effective; but remember, if time allows, you can also incorporate MULTIPLE COLORS to separate different ideas.

This will also help to demonstrate the organization of the subject. It's beneficial to use images and symbols to enhance the visual aspects of the mind map. Since our brains respond well to images, pictures, or symbols, adding in color can only help the memorization process.

The more color and images you use, the easier it will be for brain to recall (more on this in 5.2).

Take a look at the below example in order to better understand what we mean by lines, twigs, and components.

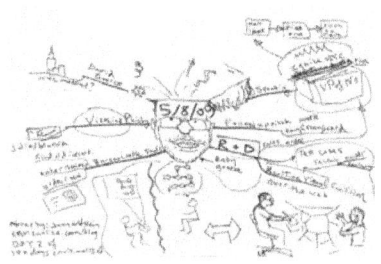

This can seem overwhelming, but the information presented in this mind map is meant to make sense to the person using it. This particular map is being used to plan out his day; therefore, he placed the date in the middle, and made his 'to do' list using texts and pictures.

Each task is connected to the main idea (the day) by 'twigs' or lines. From those, he has smaller branches that point to specifics of the task.

CONNECTIONS are an important principle in mind mapping because your brain is able to analyze the way things are interconnected. Making connections in the mind helps use to create an image or picture.

Many study techniques rely on connections and schema, and that is because the brain relies on associations to link different ideas and subjects together to create a larger system.

HEADLINES are an important principle in Mind mapping because it is easier to recall single words, phrases, and short headlines that stand out than it is to remember long strands of text.

Mind mapping allows your brain to work within its natural state, rather than forcing it to go in an unnatural direction (straight lines)

Before you begin, we have included a few important concepts to remember about Mind mapping.

This list will make it simpler for you to recall the main principals, so turn down the page corner, bookmark it, highlight it, or write the page number down as this will prove to be an important reference for you.

Use an arrow to connect one idea that flows into—or that is interconnected with—another.

Use an arrow pointing in both directions to indicate that your subjects are of equal value and that they are interrelated.

Use a free-floating box with no arrow to include a floating topic. This is typically an important idea that you want to remember, but one that is also off-topic. It basically hovers outside your map in case you need it.

Your main idea or subject is included in the middle of your map, usually enclosed in a circle to separate it from other thoughts and ideas.

Connect sub-topics to your main idea by drawing lines or branches that are connected to your arrows (if applicable)

You can circle your sub-topic if you want to, but you don't have to. You can use different colors to represent different sets of ideas.

Have fun with it!

A complete mind map can look like a tree diagram, an octopus, a map of a city, or it can be a work of art. Regardless of their aspects or characteristics, all mind maps are equally effective.

Furthermore, it is normal for mind maps to form different shapes and to be completely different because every person is unique. Often, mind maps will only make sense to those who create them.

With the help of a mind map, you can start organizing the information and the ideas needed for you to put together reports, letters, essays, poems, and lists of priorities. They can also help you to succeed in other activities, such as presentations, meetings, brainstorming sessions, and project management goals.

Using Colors, Shapes and Images

Colors

If writing things on the paper is engaging the left side of your brain, and color is working the right side, then wouldn't MORE color kick more of brain into drive?

If you have five ideas branching off of the main idea, and each of those has 3 sub points, then each idea and subsequent points should be given a color of their own.

This means that you would have a total of five colors on your mind map. Give your brain as many anchors to hold onto as possible. Associating a color with an idea will aid in committing it to memory.

Color will also make looking at it visually pleasing; greatly increasing the odds that you would actually use it to review and recall information as it was intended.

Shapes and Images

While circles are very effective in your mind map, assigning each sub point a color as well as a shape of its own will provide an additional way that your brain can hold onto the information. When working with kids, the shape of item can be drawn instead of a main idea, and the branches/lines can come directly from it.

Take a look at the mind map created by a student who was studying the components of a computer; remember that glia cell we showed you earlier? Even in its simplest form –a child's drawing-, the mind map is made to imitate the cell found within the brain.

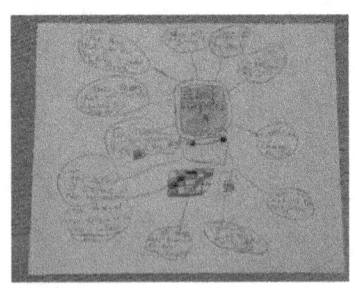

Pictures are an important principle in mind mapping because it is much easier to remember an image than it is to remember several lines of textual information.

Your brain takes shots of images as you go through your daily life and stores them in your head. You can retrieve these images at any moment you need them. Often we say to ourselves, "I know that person, I just can't remember their name." This is because your brain is designed to work in images. This is why images are such a critical part of mind mapping.

Creating a mind map

The concept of mind mapping involves creating order out of ideas, rather than leaving them in their jumbled and random state.

In general, a mind map is based on a main concept or a keyword, surrounded by five to ten ideas and their sub-points/ideas.

Mind mapping is one of the oldest techniques used for solving problems; the very nature of a mind map generates creativity.

Your sub-topics will flow from the central idea or main topic included in the middle of the page. Working outward, from the center, you will fill in the sub-topics

Start with a clear, simple picture or image at the center of the map that sums up your problem or goal. Don't worry about creating a beautiful drawing that is polished. A quick doodle works just as well.

Include letters that are clearly printed; using clear, simple phrases and easy to read print instead of scripted, sloppy characters will help you to visualize and quickly recall and retain information.

Use CAPITAL Letters, which tend to be more memorable, for important ideas and separate interconnected concepts using a combination of capitals and printed lower-case letters.

Always include keywords on lines and branches to connect thoughts and build a structure within the information included on your map.

One of the most important aspects to Mind mapping is to get ideas down on paper quickly, and put them down wherever they fit. You should **avoid holding back any thoughts or ideas that enter your mind.**

Time can play an important role in working to reach your mind mapping goals. Instead of mapping out your ideas for hours at a time, set a predetermined time limit. Your creative thoughts will flow much more readily when you are w**orking against a clock** (especially if you are able to avoid judging or filtering them).

Use arrows, lines, and icons to link your ideas together as a collective unit with distinctive differences. It doesn't matter what you use, arrows, lines, branches, or some other design that works best for you—anything that links your ideas together and supports the organization of your map will do.

If you notice that one line or branch on your mind map is drying out, or heading in a different or a new direction, **don't hesitate to move to another branch and let your mind move in that direction.**

Move through the process of mind mapping in a **place or environment that works best** for your natural thought process. Perhaps you work better alone and without distractions.

Maybe you work best at a coffee shop, in the kitchen, or in your backyard. **Go to a place that creates a pleasant atmosphere** and draws out your thoughts and ideas in a way that is most natural for you.

The most important thing is to **keep your pen firmly on the paper** and try not to allow your mind to become distracted. As a process, it takes effort, but it is time and effort well spent to develop important ideas and organize information in a productive manner.

As you go along, you may come across **new information, which can be linked** to the mind map appropriately. You might have lines or branches moving in all directions from the center; this is perfectly fine.

Sub-topics and facts will branch off of these, like branches or twigs on the trunk of a tree. It isn't necessary to worry about the structure that develops; it will evolve on its own.

To draw impactful mind maps, remember to **use short phrases** or single words. Too many words can lessen the impact of the strategies that make up mind mapping.

The shape of your mind map—or the order in which you decide to arrange your ideas—is irrelevant in relation to the basic principles presented above. As long as you take the principles outlined above into consideration, you do not have to worry about the final result.

If your mind map helps you achieve your goal, then you have done it correctly!

Creative Mind mapping

In this section, we will include ideas and tips about creative mind mapping, which can make the process of mind mapping far more enjoyable; not to mention that the finished product can be quite beautiful.

Creative mind mapping is a great way to really put this tool to optimal use. Creative maps are not only fun to make, but the finished product will help you to master the content because it will stand out to you visually.

Creative mind mapping can help you to break down creative blocks, develop visual solutions, and generate thoughts and ideas that are unique and innovative.

Creative mapping can really help you to master the overall process as a lifelong skill. In fact, mind mapping has become a revolutionary skill for artists and designers looking to challenge creative issues.

It moves the entire process to another level, but it is important to learn how to best develop your mind mapping strategies.

Below is an example of a creative mind map used to map the current system of employment. Not all aspects will make sense to every reader, but that's because it was designed to work specifically for the creator's brain. Each image, color, and even size of objects make sense in a significant way to the person who created it.

How to Produce a Creative Mind map

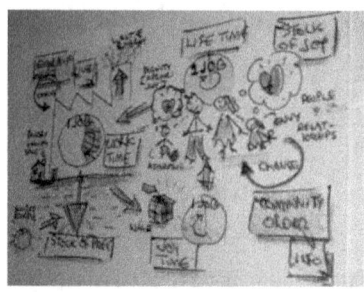

The best part about creative Mind mapping is that it's fun. To start, you will need a piece of plain paper and colored pens or pencils. The best way to orient your page is to use a landscape view so that you have plenty of space to think and move radially.

STEP ONE: **Define the problem** or main concept you are trying to explore.

In the middle of your page, sketch or draw an image that represents the creative problem you are trying to solve. Your problem could be anything client related, a product idea, your target audience, marketing plans, or an artistic concept.

Before you begin adding ideas and thoughts, consider what you are trying to achieve or develop. **Label the image in the center of your page** using one or two words that clearly define your problem.

Let your thoughts wander as you go along; the map should work with your normal thinking process, not against it. The important thing is that you are able to capture your thoughts and ideas.

The reason you place the main concept or problem in the middle of the paper is so that you have enough room to spread your thoughts and ideas across the span of the page in all different directions. This circular thinking works with our brains natural thinking as well.

As you begin to grow more confident in the use of the mind map, you may want to let your creativity extend the main idea to different positions on your map (see the example mind map below).

Step Two: Allow your creativity to take control.

This is the fun part; break out your colored pens and pencils and **draw thick lines** (these often resemble tree branches) that flow from the picture in the center of your page.

You will use each branch to draw or sketch your related thoughts and ideas.

Remember, there are no limits on how you want to develop your thoughts and ideas on paper. Many mind mappers include five to seven branches on their map, but you can include as many or as few as you want.

Look below at the example of a creative mind map. This particular one was originally created for a campaign to raise awareness of the credibility of Wikipedia. This one is computer generated and the main focus is not centered, however, I assure you this about as creative and involved as a mind map gets!

There is no limit to what you can do!

If your creative map has more of a traditional angle, then on each branch, sketch or draw symbols or pictures and include clear, one-word labels to express your key thoughts and ideas. If you are stuck, ask yourself questions related to who, what, where, when, how, and why's of your problem or concept.

For example, include ideas on each branch with labels like "audience", or "purpose". Make your mind map as visually stimulating as possible; including multiple colors to represent each branch and idea is visually exciting and helps to get the brain thinking and creating without restrictions.

Adding doodles or reference images to your map can really help you to stimulate memories. It is often more effective for this purpose than just including words.

The following is an example of mind map made following these techniques.

Step three: Associative thinking

Associative thinking is the next stage, which will help you to expand your map. To begin, **review the main keyword branches** you have already included to

come up with new key words that are connected to your main components.

These will become your sub-branches, and you can include as many of these branches as you would like.

Create each branch to resemble the branches of a tree. They can be slightly smaller than your main branches, and similarly, they grow thinner as they branch out.

For example, if you are looking to develop sub-branches for your the "audience" branch you developed earlier, you could include sub-branches that **include symbols or images** that represent each type of audience you are appealing to.

Label them based on the audience type; for instance, you could develop one sub-branch labeled single mothers, and another sub-branch labeled grandparents, and so on.

At this point, you can **continue to follow each sub-branch as you go along**, producing new ideas that are related to the audience branch, for example.

Step four: Putting it together

The final stage involves **putting all of the pieces together** to link the various elements on your page, and to continue branching out your ideas.

When you run out of new ideas, break out your colored pens and pencils to **start connecting everything together** in a way that is visually pleasing and memorable.

This stage can also help you to generate new ideas that will give your creative project a breath of fresh air.

Chapter 15: Using Colors And Images In Mind Maps

If you are interested in learning about Mind Maps and how we can use them in all we do. Its good to get a good mind map book that has step by step guides explaining the methodologies and how we can use Mind Maps to improve our productivity, planning and organization skills.

Mind Maps are being used more and more commonly, by people from all walks of life. Students use Mind Maps to learn new information, understand new concepts, and enable themselves to better recall the information later.

Many people and Business professionals use them to brainstorm ideas, make presentations to clients, and get their team organized.

Anyone can use them to enhance their creativity, and accomplish more each day by being more organized.

Mind Maps have enjoyed such popularity because they are simple to use, and they engage both sides of the brain in the learning process.

The left side of the brain is involved with rational, logical thinking, and it is what people commonly use to try to understand new concepts, and develop solutions to problems.

The right side of the brain is the artistic, creative side, and it is often neglected in intellectual, problem-solving exercises, but its involvement is just as important in learning and creativity, because using both sides of your brain helps you understand concepts more easily, and remember more of the information you have learned

The diagrammatical structure of a Mind Map, in itself, helps to involve the right hemisphere of the brain in the learning process, because a Mind Map is nothing more than a picture that contains information.

The left side of the brain is engaged by the information contained in the Map, while the right side interests itself in the Map as an image. The simplest way to do this is to use colored lines to connect the ideas in your Map; after creating all of your sub-topics, use colored lines instead of black ones to connect each sub-topic to the central idea.

Use a different color for each sub-topic, or organize the sub-topics by color-coding them; green for financial ideas, red for potential obstacles, or any other scheme you would like to use.

The power of Mind Maps to engage your right brain can also be enhanced by changing the layout or shape of the Map; for example, if you were trying to learn key facts and statistics about the fishing industry, you might want to shape the Map like a boat, or a fish. You will be able to visualize the Map in your mind, you will know how many sub-topics there were and where they were located, and you will find it much easier to remember the information.

If you were brainstorming ideas about what it would take to start up your own florist business, you could shape each sub-topic like a flower, and use different types or colors of flowers to link common themes together.

This would help you, or anyone else brainstorming with you, to keep the central idea of the florist in mind while coming up with ideas. Draw on the Map, or use clip art to illustrate it.

If you are using Mind Maps to teach, use images or graphs that will help your students understand the concepts that you are presenting to them.

By using graphs or pictures that represent the points you are trying to make, you will help them to understand the information better when it is presented, and enable easier recall later. Mind Maps can also be used as powerful motivational tools; if you want to see a 15% increase in profits, then illustrate your map of brainstormed ideas with a graph showing a 15% increase.

Chapter 16: The S.M.A.R.T.

Philosophy

A common guideline when it comes to goal setting is called the S.M.A.R.T. philosophy, which is an acronym that stands for:

Specific

Your goal must be specific. The more specific, the more likely you are to achieve it. Clarity is power. If you write down, "I want to make more money", the problem is that it doesn't clarify how much money. The same goes with, "I want to lose weight." How much weight? What percent body fat do you want to be? How do you want to look and feel? Again, the more details your goal includes, the better.

Measurable

Your goal must be something that you can measure regularly. This is a problem that most people have with setting goals. Most people set their new year resolutions, but never check in with them again. They don't have a way of measuring them consistently to see whether or not they're making progress or on track to achieving it. I personally check in with my goals and measure where I'm at weekly so I can evaluate myself and whether what I'm doing is working or not. This is another reason why your goals need to be specific. You can't measure "I want to lose weight", but you can measure "I want to lose 10 pounds."

Attainable

Your goal must be attainable. When you set the timeframe for your goal, it must be something that is realistic, which is mentioned below. If you set a goal that is impossible to attain, then you are setting yourself up for failure.

Realistic

Along with being attainable, your goal also must be realistic. I see people all the time setting goals like, "I want to make a million dollars by next month!" I used to set goals like that, as there's a few books out there that say you need to think bigger. While I agree with thinking big, sometimes too unrealistic can have damaging affects. For example, when you set a goal that is too unrealistic, what happens is you don't believe it can happen. If you don't believe you can achieve your goal, then you're not going to take any action to achieve it because you believe it's impossible! To make matters worse, when you don't achieve that million dollars in a month, you feel bad, beat yourself up, feel like a failure and then lose your confidence to set goals in the future.

Instead, I always set realistic and attainable goals. This is how I did it with my internet businesses. When I was making $30/month, I set the goal of making only $100 the next month. Once I achieved that, I would feel good, proud about myself, celebrate, and then set the next goal at $300/month. At this point, I already have confidence and momentum because I had achieved the previous goal that I set. Once I achieved $300/month, I set the goal of $500/month. Then $1000/month. $2000/month. Eventually to $5000/month, $8200/month, $10,000/month, $12,000/month, and so fourth.

I simply slowly increased the amount of earnings I wanted to make over a period of time and gained tremendous confidence and momentum while doing it!

Timeline

Last, but not least, you need a timeline. There's a lot of benefit and power in having a timeline for your goal. A timeline is what gets you to actually complete the goal. If you don't have a timeline and the time for completion is open-ended, then who's to say you will ever achieve it?

You want to create PRESSURE on yourself. As the saying goes, "Pressure creates diamonds."

Think about when you were going to school. In school, they teach you the power of having a timeline or deadline. The teachers assign homework and projects for you that you must complete by a certain due date. Since the teacher assigns a date, you will ALWAYS get the homework or project done, as there is a consequence to not completing it. If there was no due date, you most likely wouldn't get it done. You may even have left your homework or studying to the last minute, as I always did, but you'd ALWAYS get it done, even if it meant staying up all night to complete it.

This S.M.A.R.T. philosophy has proven to be useful for me when setting my goals and achieving them. As mentioned, most people when they send me their goals are lacking these simple steps that make all the difference.

Chapter 17: Mind Map Techniques

Once you are able to understand how Mind Mapping works, it is important for you to know the different Mind Map techniques that will help you create effective diagrams. Below are several techniques that you can adapt once you start creating Mind Maps of your own:

Keep it simple

Use simple yet catchy phrases. Keep them short and simple. Too many words can clutter your diagram and may end up confusing you and your target audience or readers. Single word statements can be very powerful and motivating. The key is in finding and selecting the right words that can generate the intended impact. Focus on positive and encouraging words or phrases. Allow the words that you select to speak to you and to your readers. They should be words that you value. Keep them light and direct to the point. Don't beat around the bush and focus the message that you wish to convey.

Connect the dots

Use arrows to show how each idea is connected to the other. Make those arrows definitive and precise. Keep in mind that your Mind Map can branch out to many ideas. It can grow so big that you and your readers may end up getting lost in the sea of ideas that you have generated. An idea from the other side of a map is most likely going to be related to the idea on the other side. Be sure to use what are called cross-linkages to be able to show the connection. Doing so will allow you and your readers to follow the flow of thoughts in your Mind Map.

Print it

Words play a crucial role in an effective Mind Map. Therefore, it is important that you print your words carefully to ensure that you are conveying the right message. Remember that you are using in your Mind

Map simple yet powerful and compelling words. You would not want those words to lose their potency by writing them in barely legible forms. Use bold, neat and clear fonts. The written words should be easy on the eyes. You should be able to immediately read and understand them. The meaning of each word should register right away in your mind.

Play with colors

Use colors when creating your Mind Map. Play with them and don't be shy about using them. Colors can help you emphasize your points. You can use colors to highlight specific ideas that are of importance. A vivid color like red often symbolizes urgency and importance while cool colors like blue can signify acceptable but less urgent ideas. Colors can immediately catch someone's attention therefore, it is important that you use them wisely and strategically in your Mind Maps. The play of colors is very useful in helping you commit the diagram you created to your memory. The various colors can serve as memory triggers, which will enable you to recall specific parts of your diagram in great detail.

Experiment with imagery

Don't be afraid to use images. Be creative and experiment with the use of photos, icons and even animations. Use them to represent your thoughts and ideas. Find images that suit the message that you are trying to project. The use of images can also encourage and motivate you to follow your Mind Map. Use images to remind you of the goals that you need to achieve. Use them to warn you of the things that you need to avoid. Use them to show you where to go next. Don't be shy when using images just as long as you see to it that the images you use are related to your subject.

Let it flow

Lastly, allow your thoughts and creativity to flow every time you create a task map. Don't limit yourself to what you see on the books and online pages. Allow your mind to generate those ideas and follow them wherever they may lead you. Let your ideas multiply. Our minds have an unimaginable capacity to produce ideas for as long as we are alive. Don't try to stop them. Allow them to flow. There is no wrong or right idea. Everything matters. Maybe one idea is more important than the other but that does not diminish their value. Acknowledge and be grateful for all of them.

Chapter 18: Mind Map Software

Mind mapping is a creative activity which begins when you write a central idea or subject and then draw lines and link into different "nodes," each of them with a new word or concept connected to the first one.

Easy enough.

So you have a blank piece of paper on a globe, but digitalising the method makes the process simple so versatile.

The chances are not limited to the size of your paper with a digital mental map and can quickly shift ideas with little effort.

We have reviewed several hundred mind mapping devices, and here we present the 11 best to help you find the right way to chart your mind.

What Makes Software for Great Mind Mapping?

Each of the best mind mapping tools has unique advantages, but at least they all have the following: Free linen.

If you have limits of your mind mapping canvas, your imagination can be only limited because you run out of space.

Even if you can't see the entire map at once, you can imagine an infinite canvas until you are finished.

Capable of attaching files.

Often the text is not enough to express your thoughts, or you want an additional file to include in your brainstorming.

You may attach links, images and some other files to your mind map in all the best mind mapping apps.

Attributes of collaboration

Mind map applications built on the cloud should facilitate cooperation and comment on the canvas for multiple users.

All of the better desktop apps provide for sufficient sharing / syncing of cloud data through platforms so that multiple users can access and refresh the mind map.

Saving and exportability. Such apps all allow you to save and re-edit your map in future, and they all provide the ability to share or export maps online.

What's Inside

It sounds futuristic and somewhat frightening, particularly when you finish inserting the word tech.

Mind mapping software.

It indicates that the enigmatic human brain will occupy the deep regions of the.

Maybe for dangerous reasons.

It could even make a good sci-fi film story!

Naturally, mind mapping isn't that frightening; indeed, many find that this is only the technique they need to help them understand the subject they try to master.

It is the practice of arranging the various information items inside the mind in a non-linear way, so you can see links between objects where the relations were not always apparent.

Mind mapping helps people within their brains to step into a computer program where the software transforms it into a representation allowing people to see it all at once.

So, what is a mind map exactly?

A visual chart is just a sketch. It can be used to represent anything and frequently adopted for charting diagram

☐ Concepts

☐ Ideas

☐ Aims

☐ Tasks

☐ Emotions

☐ Problems/Solutions

or team building activities or personal creative activities.

A consultant might, for example, ask a buyer to generate a mental map around the term ' fear,' or a boss could ask the employee to create a spiritual plan about the expression ' increased profit.

It is a standard brainstorming method and is of great interest to people who do not necessarily function linearly.

Mind mapping software can help the mind mapping process immeasurably. The use of a software program has many advantages, rather than merely trying to do it by hand.

More Choices.

This program can make your diagrams in ways you couldn't imagine, but it could be beneficial to you. Colours, shapes, contact points and storing of additional materials all lead to your great mind map.

3-D.

It is the most recent development of the maps. If thoughts need not be linear, why should they be two-dimensional?

Greater memory.

The computer can remember more than you can, so more can be drawn into your mind. it drastically reduces the chance that you are on your forehead and say, I've forgotten that!" Software for mind mapping can organise and provide easy access to much more material than the human mind can envelop itself.

An entire information network.

You will find links, records, files, attachments and visuals with Mind Mapping that you could never see yourself.

Mind mapping is an old concept, but the software for mental mapping takes it to the 21st century.

Using this method, you will visualise, prepare, coordinate, discover, analyse, arrange and envision more possibilities than you otherwise might.

It's an invaluable tool that anybody can have, and of course, more tools mean more and better.

Why Mind Mapping Software Beats Paper

Why Mind Mapping Software Beats Paper

The idea of mind mapping has always been there. In reality, the mind maps can be sketch back to the 3rd century Porphyry of Tyros.

Nevertheless, in the 1960s, Allan M. Collins and M created the new mind map. Ross Quillian. Thanks to mind mapping tools, they evolved even further today in 2009.

Instead of paper versions, the use of mind mapping software offers many benefits.

When an abstract diagram set on paper, there is no way to rearrange concepts without manually editing them and re-writing them or starting a new one.

You can organise your thoughts several times with mind mapping tools until they are just where you want them, which prevents you a lot of energy and dissatisfaction.

Another great feature of mind mapping apps is that you can put information in collapsible concept trees that can extend as appropriate.

Paper-drawn mind maps do not allow this flexibility and finally, look very disruptive and jumbled.

There is no limit to how much information you can place in the collapsible topic trees with the software.

It may contain Word or Excel documents, links to websites, e-mails, lists, etc.

It reduces the amount of documentation to be done by the customer.

Everything is on the online mind map, just one click away. What a great advantage!

You can also export the ideas and information to other applications through mind mapping tools, if appropriate.

It helps you to use a diagram for any project by arranging and prioritising the details before it is essential applications like display, project management or word processing apps.

You can even send the chart to other team members where they can take it and add information.

Finally, this software enables you to present your ideas to a room full of people at once on an LCD projector and screen.

While this is comparable to PowerPoint, it isn't identical because mind mapping software allows you to add information quickly and immediately to your chart in real-time during your meeting or brainstorming session.

PowerPoint presentations do not offer this much-required versatility.

The advantages of utilising mind mapping apps do not limit to the ones listed above.

There are many more benefits to be discovered. The versatility in mind mapping tools has opened the door to a variety of uses of mind maps, from the creation of a business plan, project management to the tracking of your personal goals and writing books.

Mind mapping software facilitates the organisation of your thoughts and ideas in virtually every forthcoming project or event and saves time and productivity in a convenient place.

Mind Mapping Software Helps Personal Development

It is no secret that mind mapping has all kinds of technical and business applications, but fewer people realise that it can be a massive help in personal development.

In their personal lives, mind mapping software can help people.

It enables them to organise and organise things around them, such as schedules, calendars and tasks, such as ideas, feelings and memories.

Here are just a variety of ways mind mapping apps will help you develop yourself.

Management Of Time.

Time seems to be flowing linearly, but that does not mean that our goals automatically come into place.

Mind map software can help us find out what needs to perform, who is there to do it, and how we can make our time a priority for our families to achieve the best results.

Memories.

It often seems like memories are lost, but typically they're there, somewhere under the water. Mind maps will help you create websites with similar ideas and emotions.

Making Decisions.

Most companies and institutions use concept mapping software, but individuals and families can use it as well.

With this software, each choice and its possible results can map quickly and clearly. It is also a useful technique for teaching children who face difficult decisions in their lives.

Question Management.

Mind maps can help you move from a place where you react to problems to a place where you change your circumstances creatively. With the aid of mind mapping tools, more and more ideas become apparent.

Emotional Health.

Most clinicians utilise mental visualisation techniques to help their patients explore their feelings, but you can do it for yourself as well.

You are unhappy, frustrated, unhappy? Work it in a map of your mind, and you will find new insights that might surprise you.

Set The Target.

It seems like a linear process to D, and you go through steps A, B and C-but many creative approaches are available to identify and plan for your goals that linear thinking is not equipping to reveal.

Once you start your ideas into your mind, mapping software, new options and new opportunities are many clearers.

Spiritual Development.

Mind mapping can help you, of course, to identify your spiritual values and goals, but it can be even more so.

Mind maps can be a form of prayer or medicine themselves. Through this strategy, you will ponder the identity or role of your Supreme Being.

It would help if you worshipped every aspect of the divine character as it occurs in your mind's depths.

Meditation can be difficult for those who fidget stillness, but if your account can relax by mapping your mind, then you can float on spiritual paths free.

Anxiety Or Unfair Treatment.

Sometimes it is a place to express all of these negative emotions. Use your mind mapping program and type them in to send them a deep breath to press the delete button. See.

Go! And that's all the terror.

The use of mental maps and mind mapping is practically unlimited.

Take some time to learn how this reliable and unique resource will help you improve your life.

Conclusion

After reading this book, you will be able to understand mind-mapping better, and how you could use them not just for self-improvement but also for reaching your business or career goals.

The next step is to start practicing the mind-mapping techniques mentioned in this book. You do not have to do all of them in a single day. Just try to integrate them in your life gradually, and soon, you'll find yourself being able to organize your thoughts and see things clearer. If you find yourself having a hard time starting, take a look at the mind-mapping examples mentioned.

www.ingramcontent.com/pod-product-compliance
Lightning Source LLC
Chambersburg PA
CBHW071441070526
44578CB00001B/186